D1559014

ESSENTIALS
of Banking

Essentials Series

The Essentials Series was created for busy business advisory and corporate professionals. The books in this series were designed so that these busy professionals can quickly acquire knowledge and skills in core business areas.

Each book provides need-to-have fundamentals for those professionals who must:

- Get up to speed quickly, because they have been promoted to a new position or have broadened their responsibility scope
- Manage a new functional area
- Brush up on new developments in their area of responsibility
- Add more value to their company or clients

Other books in this series include:

Essentials of Accounts Payable, Mary S. Schaeffer
Essentials of Balanced Scorecard, Mohan Nair
Essentials of Business Process Outsourcing, Robert L. Click and Thomas N. Duening
Essentials of Cash Flow, H. A. Schaeffer, Jr.
Essentials of Corporate Fraud, Tracey Coenen
Essentials of Corporate Governance, Sanjay Anand
Essentials of Corporate Performance Measurement, George T. Friedlob, Lydia L.F. Schleifer, and Franklin J. Plewa, Jr.
Essentials of Cost Management, Joe and Catherine Stenzel
Essentials of Credit, Collections, and Accounts Receivable, Mary S. Schaeffer
Essentials of Financial Analysis, George T. Friedlob and Lydia L.F. Schleifer
Essentials of Financial Risk Management, Karen A. Horcher
Essentials of Intellectual Property, Paul J. Lerner and Alexander I. Poltorak
Essentials of Knowledge Management, Bryan Bergeron
Essentials of Managing Treasury, Karen A. Horcher
Essentials of Patents, Andy Gibbs and Bob DeMatteis
Essentials of Sarbanes-Oxley, Sanjay Anand
Essentials of Supply Chain Management, 2nd Edition, Michael Hugos
Essentials of Trademarks and Unfair Competition, Dana Shilling
Essentials of XBRL, Bryan Bergeron

For more information on any of the above titles, please visit www.wiley.com

ESSENTIALS
of Banking

Deborah K. Dilley

John Wiley & Sons, Inc.

This book is printed on acid-free paper. ♾

Published by John Wiley & Sons, Inc., Hoboken, New Jersey.

Published simultaneously in Canada.

For general information on our other products and services, or technical support, please contact our Customer Care Department within the United States at 800-762-2974, outside the United States at 317-572-3993 or fax 317-572-4002.

Wiley also publishes its books in a variety of electronic formats. Some content that appears in print may not be available in electronic books.

For more information about Wiley products, visit our Web site at http://www.wiley.com.

Library of Congress Cataloging-in-Publication Data:

Dilley, Deborah K.
Essentials of banking / Deborah K. Dilley.
p. cm. – (Essentials series)
Includes index.
ISBN 978-0-470-17088-5 (pbk.)
1. Banks and banking—United States. 2. Banking law—United States. I. Title.
HG2491.D55 2008
332.10973–dc22 2007048498

Printed in the United States of America

10 9 8 7 6 5 4 3 2 1

To my parents, Rosemary and Walter Dilley

Acknowledgments

This book would never have been created without David Martin, John Voorhees, Lucas Freeman and Ken Rosenberg--the guiding forces behind Sage Online Learning, Ltd. Without them; I might never have sold Sage's online library of courses to SmartPros, Ltd–the serendipity that led to this book! Thanks also to Halley Porter, Eric & Felicia Anderson and Jack Robson for the early years—your contributions stay in my heart.

This book was born from a belief that "one" book was needed for bankers and lay people alike that covered the essential elements of banking–products and services, compliance, business development, supervision, and marketing–all in one place. Thanks to Jack Fingerhut, President, SmartPros, Ltd for agreeing with this concept and introducing me to John DeRemigis at Wiley & Sons. John shepherded me through the process of creating the bones of the book and encouraged me to refine my ideas into a concrete structure.

At Wiley thank you also to Judy Howarth, Associate Editor, for guiding me through the manuscript process—an incredible challenge I am sure! You did what was needed–nudging and urgent prodding–whatever it took to move the book forward. Natasha Andrews-Noel, Production Editor at Wiley carried the book through production without missing a beat. I appreciate her clear communication style and "matter of fact" taskmaster, traits.

A lion's share of the thanks goes to Julie Todd at SmartPros who juggled her full time "regular" job with the huge job of managing the manuscript's word processing. Julie, Mark Tilley and Jack Fingerhut also spent many hours on the sometimes-tedious review of the manuscript and I am grateful for their patience and suggestions. I'd like to also acknowledge the original authors and contributors to the online courses. These courses laid the foundation for this book and some of the content is incorporated as it originally appeared.

I'd like to express my appreciation to my good friend, Ken Wachtel of Leland, Parachini, Steinberg, Matzger & Melnick, LLP of San Francis co for reviewing the book—some of it on vacation and in the midst of running for Mill Valley City Council (he won). Thanks to Jason and Leah, Leslie, Tammy, Michelle, Jacquie, Pam and Steffie for your encouragement.

And most important thanks to my son, Kenny and husband, Ken for enduring the many late nights and grumpy mornings as deadlines came and went. Your love, support and sense of humor got me through—as always

About the Author

Deborah K. Dilley, was President and CEO of Sage Online Learning, Inc., prior to its acquisition by SmartPros, Ltd. Ms. Dilley, who joined SmartPros in February 2006 as Director of SmartPros Banking is a seasoned financial services executive and senior manager with a successful two-decade career in the banking, high tech, and corporate training industries. Prior to founding Sage, Ms. Dilley served as Executive Vice President of Field Operations at an early-stage Internet startup offering content to the financial services industry. Ms. Dilley brings an in-depth knowledge of the regulatory demands and training requirements of the financial services industry as well as the technical know-how to deliver online learning reliably and effectively.

During her career in the financial services industry, Ms. Dilley held various senior management positions at Bankers Trust Company (now Deutsche Bank), First Interstate Bank, and Wells Fargo Bank and also served as Executive Vice President of Omega Performance Corporation, where she created and launched a new multimedia division delivering custom training solutions for customers such as State Farm, Fidelity Investments, Delta Airlines, and J. P. Morgan.

About SmartPros: SmartPros Banking is part of the Financial Services division of SmartPros Ltd. SmartPros, which was founded in 1981, is a leading provider of online Continuing Professional Education for professionals in banking, insurance, brokerage, accounting and finance. For more information on SmartPros and its online courses visit the SmartPros website at www.smartpros.com.

Contents

Preface

You don't need to be a banker to realize the impact of the banking system and its repercussions in our everyday work and personal worlds. Whoever you are, and whatever your interest in learning about banking, you are participating in exciting times. Whether you are a teller in a bank located in a small agricultural community in the Midwest, a management trainee in a regional bank with offices throughout the Southeast, an employee in a bank that has locations across the United States and several foreign countries, or someone who simply needs to gain a better understanding of banking concepts, this book will introduce you to the world of banking by looking at the industry both from a historical and present-day perspective.

But what about the future? What will banking look like in 5, 10, or even 20 years? This is a tough question to answer, but we'll explore the possibilities. Most certainly, banking in the future will be driven by competition in the business of banking and reinvented as banking functions continue to become fragmented among different types of financial institutions and nontraditional financial partners.

Trends in banking affect the future but, even more, they affect what you do today. More than looking at the future of banking, this book will be an invaluable reference for you in your day-to-day job responsibilities. We explore the basics of banking so that you will understand the various banking products and services that exist and the role of banks in financial intermediation. We also look at all aspects of the regulatory environment that surrounds the banking industry. This is the environment that provides the integrity that allows the banking system to operate as seamlessly as it does.

We also examine how the focus in banking has shifted from a historical product-driven focus to a customer-driven focus and how banking is using multiple channels to service customers rather than relying only on banking offices. And we explore how cross-industry affiliations may significantly change the face of banking in the next several decades. We also define banking jargon and common acronyms and place them into context.

In the end, you will come away with a greater understanding of banking functions and products and their relation to other financial business activities and be able to apply your knowledge in useful ways regardless of your chosen career path. You'll have a guide that you can refer to that contains information about all of the relevant facts of banking in one place.

CHAPTER 1

Banking 101: Understanding the Basics

After reading this chapter, you will be able to:

- Understand the origin of banking and how it has evolved.
- Explain the role of banks in the creation of money.
- Discuss the essential elements of electronic banking and funds transfers.
- Recognize the role of banks in financial intermediation.
- Describe the range of products and services offered by banks.
- Understand how financial products and services satisfy the needs of customers.

What Is a Bank?

A *bank* is defined by Merriam-Webster's online dictionary (www.merriamwebster.com) as "an establishment for the custody, loan, exchange, or issue of money, for the extension of credit, and for facilitating the transmission of funds."

While they are simple to describe, the roles of banks, bankers, and banking are—for some—not as simple to understand.

"Banking" can be defined as "the business of banking," a vibrant business that continually evolves to meet the latest financial needs and economic conditions. In order to understand how banking evolves, it is important to gain a broad understanding of financial concepts, fundamental banking functions, and the banking business in a technology-driven world.

From Barter to Payment Systems

Money is the basis of banking. And the basis of money is the need for a substitute for directly bartering for everything we need. "Barter" is defined as trading without the use of money—and it can be traced back to the very origin of civilization. Can you imagine how our economy would operate if we didn't use money? You would either have to be completely self-sufficient or have to produce a good or service that you could trade for whatever you could not produce yourself. Most of us would spend our time making almost everything we needed (including growing food, building shelter, and making clothes) or working at a specialty that others needed so we could trade for many of the necessities of life. The specialties would be few. Our technological advances would be restricted by an incredibly inefficient system of exchanging goods and services.

The development of money was a significant advance over barter as a payment system. But today we have extended the concept of payment systems way beyond the original concept of money. One of the first steps into more sophisticated payment systems was the development of checks and checking accounts.

Money is a symbol of value, and checks are a symbol of money. We give another person a check when we want to give him or her money. The other person then takes that check and sends it through the check clearing system so that the money it represents is transferred from us to him or her.

Believe it or not, prior to the age of computers, banking employees posted transactions on individual account cards. Banks had to close for business early in the afternoon so that several hours could be devoted to recording and reconciling the day's transactions.

The early computer systems used in banking seemed like a tremendous advance over manual systems. But today they seem like pocket calculators compared to the computing power that the banking industry and customers depend on and, frankly, take for granted.

Computers have changed the face and complexion of the banking business. Computers have changed how customers use banking services, how banks operate internally, and how banks interact with the rest of the financial system.

Technology has revolutionized banking and continues to do so at a fiercely accelerating speed. Computers, the Internet, mobile technology, wireless access, and other improved communication systems give banking great flexibility and efficiency. All of this growth continues to create new opportunities to reinvent banks and, in particular, banking careers.

Banking also fulfills a valuable role in society by:

- Playing a key role in financial intermediation
- Creating financial products and services that benefit businesses and consumers
- Driving a thriving financial system regulated by state and federal governments
- Facilitating the creation of money
- Being involved in the transfer of funds
- Reinventing the financial future—the future of banking

In order to understand the business of banking, it is useful to understand one of its key elements—financial intermediation.

Bank's Role in Financial Intermediation

Financial intermediation is an important role in banking. The term "financial intermediation" means accepting funds from one source (such as savings customers) and using the money to make loans or other investments. Essentially, financial intermediation means acting as a go-between for individuals or businesses that have extra money and individuals or businesses that want to borrow money.

Each person or business with extra funds could try to find a borrower on its own, but the process would be time-consuming and difficult. Can you imagine how difficult it would be to find another person who would want to borrow the exact amount of your savings for the length of time you want to lend it?

Financial intermediation is a business activity that supplies a service by pooling funds from many different sources and advancing loans and making investments. The people and businesses that supply the funds receive interest or services for allowing their funds to be pooled and loaned out or invested. The borrowers pay interest for the privilege of borrowing money they use to generate income or meet other goals.

Another way to understand financial intermediation is to compare it to another type of intermediation. Consider how a blood bank operates. A blood bank finds healthy individuals and arranges for them to donate blood. The blood bank then processes the blood and makes it available to hospitals. The blood bank does not actually use the blood; it simply acts as a channel (or intermediary) between the donors and the hospitals.

Just as the blood bank functions between the donor and recipient of blood, a bank acts as an intermediary between those with extra money and those who want to borrow money. It is a financial intermediary. This is one of the unique characteristics of financial institutions, and of banks in particular—their role as financial intermediaries.

Banking and the "Creation" of Money

Banking plays the most critical role in the "creation" of money—no, not by cranking up the presses and printing money. Banks do not print currency. What we mean by the "creation of money" is this: The financial system "creates money" by expanding the supply of money through deposit and loan transactions. Exhibit 1.1 is an example of how it works.

EXHIBIT 1.1

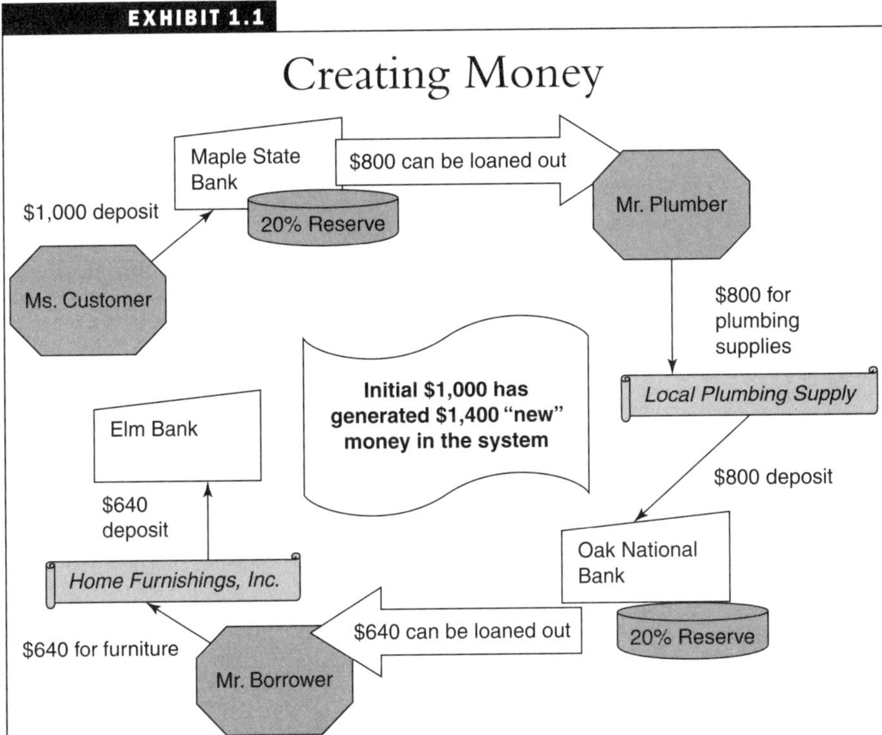

Assume that Carol Customer puts $1,000 in a checking account at Maple State Bank. The bank must set aside part of this money as reserves and can then loan out the remainder.

The Federal Reserve System establishes reserve requirements. Reserve requirements are usually fairly low, but, for this example, assume they are 20 percent of the deposit. This would mean that $800 of the deposit could be loaned out.

Paul Plumber, a Maple Bank customer, needs to borrow money and draws on a line of credit in the amount of $800. He writes out a check for the $800 and gives it to Local Plumbing Supply to purchase materials for a bathroom-remodeling project he has been hired to complete.

(continued)

EXHIBIT 1.1 (CONTINUED)

Local Plumbing Supply deposits the check to its checking account at Oak National Bank. Oak National Bank can also lend out these funds (after setting aside a portion for reserves).

Bill Borrower, a customer of Oak National Bank, draws on his home equity line of credit in the amount of $640. He uses the funds to purchase furniture from Home Furnishings, Inc.

Home Furnishings, Inc. then deposits this money in its checking account at Elm Bank.

This cycle of deposits and loans continues to "create" additional money with each set of transactions. The initial deposit of $1,000 has generated "new" money in the amount of $1,440 in the financial system.

In addition to the creation of money, banking plays an important part in the economy by providing for payment mechanisms or methods to transfer funds. Cash is the historical basis for trading goods and services in our country, but today most consumers or businesses use other methods to transfer funds from one person or business to another.

The traditional system historically is the use of checks and checking accounts. Our payment systems, however, have evolved to include other systems such as credit cards, debit cards, paperless checks, and electronic transactions (such as payments that are automatically deducted from checking accounts) to give consumers and businesses many other alternatives to cash. With the advent of Internet banking systems, the range of choices continues to expand.

Satisfying Customers' Needs—Banking Is a Service Business

While banks play a critical role in financial intermediation and in the creation of money, banking's primary focus is the satisfaction of customers' financial needs. Banking services satisfy financial needs such as:

- Earning a return on idle funds
- Borrowing money to achieve goals

- Preventing losses
- Managing money conveniently and efficiently

To be successful, banking must meet the financial needs of customers. But most customers need assistance to wade through the bewildering array of banking products and services. Many customers are not aware of all the different services available and may not have a good understanding of whether a particular service would be useful to them. Often customers are overwhelmed at the vast array of products and services. Banking professionals are the link between these products, services, and customers.

Bankers act as interpreters between the banking products and services and help customers evaluate their financial needs. Bankers suggest services that meet those needs. An important part of the job of a banker is to promote banking products to customers in a sales consultant capacity, not as a cashier. In other words, bankers help customers select the right services for them rather than simply ringing up the sale.

High Tech versus High Touch

Banking went through revolutionary changes when computers were introduced many years ago. Today, if you are reading this book, it is quite likely that you use a computer to connect to the Internet on a regular basis, so you are already aware of the powerful effect of electronic communication in our society.

Some people would argue that technology is reducing the human element in banking ("high tech" versus "high touch"). While this is true, technology is also enriching the human interaction in banking. Technology reduces boring tasks or processing of simple transactions that aren't "high touch" anyway. What technology is doing for the high-touch side of banking is making sure that interactions between customers and banking professionals are valuable for both sides.

Customers can use automated systems such as ATMs, online banking, wireless access, and telephone banking programs to process transactions quickly and get basic information. When their needs extend beyond these mechanical aspects of banking, the banking professional is there to help with the real questions, such as which checking account would be lowest cost for the customer or which loan plan would best meet the customer's needs. Helping customers with these needs is also more rewarding and satisfying for most banking professionals.

Over the years, various banking products have been developed as an outgrowth of the bank's role in financial intermediation. Many years ago, few types of banking products and services existed—primarily checking accounts and commercial loans provided to businesses and consumers. Over time, however, the number and variety of products and services have increased dramatically.

Banking Products and Services

Let's look at these products and services a little closer. To help you understand financial intermediation and the role of the bank, we define common bank products and services, including banking deposit accounts and various types of loans and lines of credit. We also discuss various other types of accounts, such as cash management and retirement accounts.

The following categories of products and services are explained:

- Deposit and transaction accounts such as:
  - Checking accounts
  - Savings accounts
  - Certificates of deposit
  - Money market accounts

- Loans and credit accounts such as:
  - Real estate loans

    - Installment loans
    - Credit cards
    - Commercial loans
    - Construction loans
    - Agricultural loans
- Other services such as:
    - Retirement plans
    - Cash management services
    - Funds transfer services
    - Payment processing
    - Debit cards

Deposits

Traditional banking deposit products can be divided into four categories:

1. Transaction accounts
2. Savings accounts
3. Certificate accounts
4. Other

The features of these accounts vary considerably depending on the type of account, its restrictions, and the specific policies of the bank where they are offered. A common characteristic of these accounts is deposit insurance provided by the Federal Deposit Insurance Corporation (FDIC), which allows customers to conduct day-to- day business and keep their funds in a safe place.

Transaction Accounts

Transaction accounts are defined as deposit accounts on which customers can write an unlimited number of checks. These types of account include:

- Interest-earning checking accounts
- Non-interest-earning checking accounts

Customers use transaction accounts for daily expenses because the funds are easily accessed and checks are a widely accepted method of payment.

Customers may need to maintain a minimum balance in a checking account. Due to the transactional nature of these accounts, the maintenance and processing costs of these accounts are higher than other deposit accounts. Therefore, customers may need to pay monthly and other fees to use the accounts. Also, the interest paid on interest-earning checking accounts is usually a low rate.

Savings Accounts

Savings accounts are interest-earning deposit accounts that usually have few restrictions on deposits and withdrawals. Two types of savings accounts offered most frequently are regular accounts and money market deposit accounts (MMDAs).

Regular savings accounts usually pay a low rate of interest and require a minimum balance. Customers often use regular savings accounts for emergency funds and to supplement the funds maintained in a checking account. Regular savings accounts are often the first account individuals open when they begin saving money beyond their daily needs.

Money market deposit accounts offer higher rates of interest that usually fluctuate according to changes in interest rates offered on investments available from other sources. MMDAs require a higher minimum balance than regular savings accounts and customers can write only a limited number of checks each month.

With MMDAs, customers can make deposits at any time and can make unlimited withdrawals by mail or in person; however, MMDAs are not intended to operate as a checking account. As a result, there are restrictions on the number of transfers allowed per month (electronic or check). The benefit of an MMDA is a higher rate of interest with relatively easy access to the funds. Customers may use an MMDA to hold large amounts of cash temporarily between investments. For example, a customer could receive an inheritance and place the funds in an MMDA while making decisions about how else to invest it.

Certificate Accounts

The third category of deposit accounts is certificate accounts. Certificate accounts are accounts that typically require a higher minimum balance and offer higher interest rates for a fixed period of time or term. Interest rates are often fixed for the term and therefore produce a predictable return.

A critical feature of certificates is a monetary penalty on early withdrawal. If the customer redeems the certificate before the end of the agreed-upon term (the maturity date), the customer must pay a penalty (at the bank's option) that is often based on the interest rate of the account (e.g., an amount equal to 90 days of interest).

Certificates may be negotiable or nonnegotiable. Negotiable certificates can be sold and resold to other businesses or individuals. Nonnegotiable certificates can be presented for payment only by the original owner. In general, customers use these accounts to hold funds for long-term goals.

Other Types of Accounts

Banking includes other types of deposit accounts, such as holiday club accounts or vacation club accounts, but these are often variations of the accounts just described.

Loans and Other Credit Services

Loans and other credit services are an important source of income for banks. There are two major categories of loans: business and consumer.

Business loans can be secured or unsecured and are primarily classified into three categories:

1. Short term
2. Long term
3. Line of credit

Short-term business loans typically have a term of less than one year and may be used for purposes such as purchasing inventory or for a seasonal need (see Exhibit 1.2).

Long-term business loans are made for a term longer than one year and may be used for purposes such as expanding a business or purchasing equipment. They are usually repaid from business income in installments (see Exhibit 1.3).

A line of credit is essentially a preapproved credit limit against which the business borrows. A line of credit can be closed or open end. In a closed-end line of credit, the business borrows and repays the funds within a certain time limit. In an open-end line of credit, the business can borrow any amount up to the approved limit, make repayments, and borrow again up to the limit.

Loans can be secured or unsecured. A secured loan is one in which an asset, such as inventory or property, is pledged against repayment of the loan. For example, a secured line of credit used to purchase inventory can be secured by that same inventory. An unsecured line of credit used to purchase the inventory is not secured by the inventory; rather, the line of credit is granted primarily because of the good credit history of the business.

Consumer loans can be divided into two categories: installment credit and mortgage loans.

Installment credit is essentially a loan or credit account on which the payments (including interest) are made at regular intervals.

If the interest rate is fixed for a set term (such as a car loan), the payments are for a fixed amount, and the loan amount and interest are fully repaid by the end of the term.

EXHIBIT 1.2

Short-term Business Loans

Example A

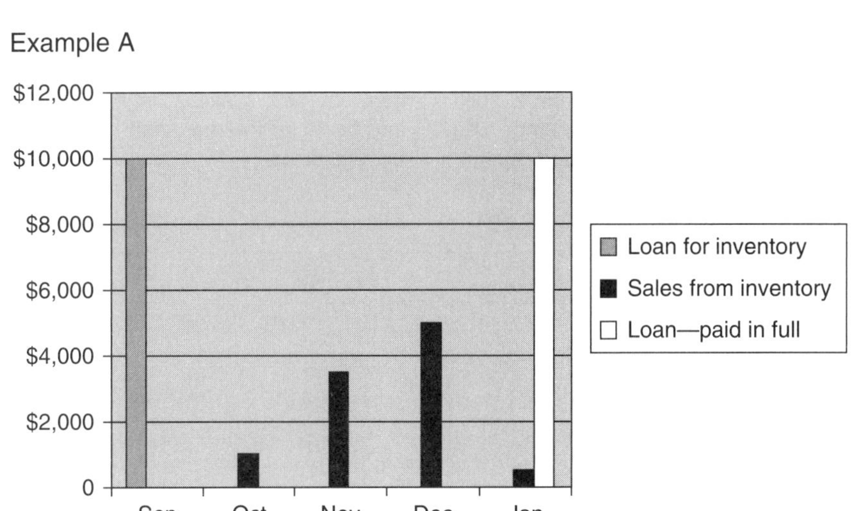

A business obtains a loan to purchase a large inventory shortly before the end-of-year holiday season. The items are sold during the season, and the loan is repaid in a lump sum.

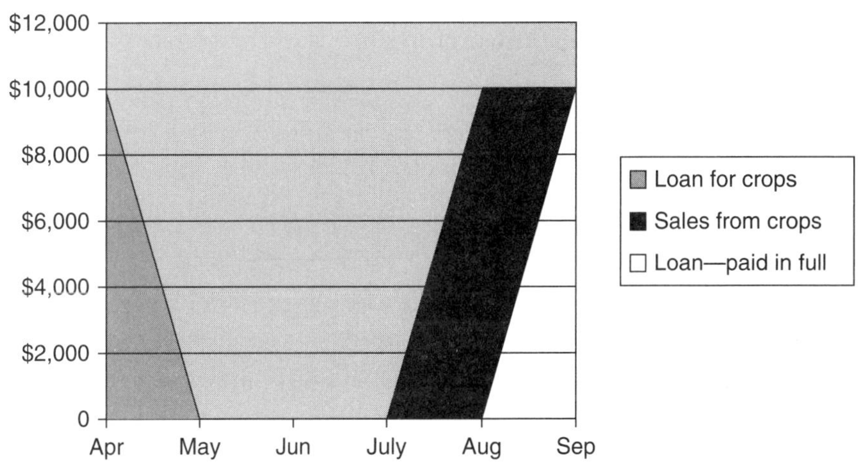

A farm obtains a loan to purchase seed and fertilizer at the beginning of the growing season. The loan is repaid when the harvested crops are sold.

EXHIBIT 1.3

Long-term Business Loans

Example A

A business has outgrown its current location and the owner needs to build an addition or a new building. The additional income generated by the expansion of the business is a source of installment payments on the loan.

Example B

A farm needs to purchase large equipment or new grain storage facilities and finances the purchase through a long-term loan.

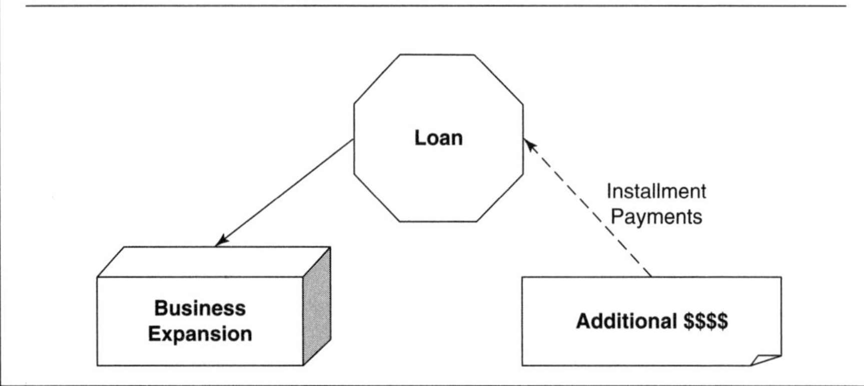

Installment credit can be secured or unsecured (see Exhibits 1.4 and 1.5).

Loans with real estate as the security for loan repayment are commonly called *mortgage loans*, however in some states real estate transactions are executed through a *deed of trust*. In either case, a customer usually obtains a loan to purchase real property. Loans are usually for a fixed term of 30 years with monthly payments. Interest rates can be fixed or adjustable.

A homeowner can also obtain a *home equity loan* (also commonly referred to as a second mortgage) against the portion of the home's value that he or she owns (the homeowner's equity).

Equity is determined by subtracting the outstanding balance of the loan(s) from the current value of the home. The formula is:

Current value of home − Outstanding balance of real estate loan(s)

= Equity

EXHIBIT 1.4

Secured Installment Loan

Bob could have an installment car loan with a 48-month term and monthly payments of $500. At the end of the 48 months, Bob has paid back the amount loaned to him plus interest. While the loan is outstanding, the car is the security for the loan.

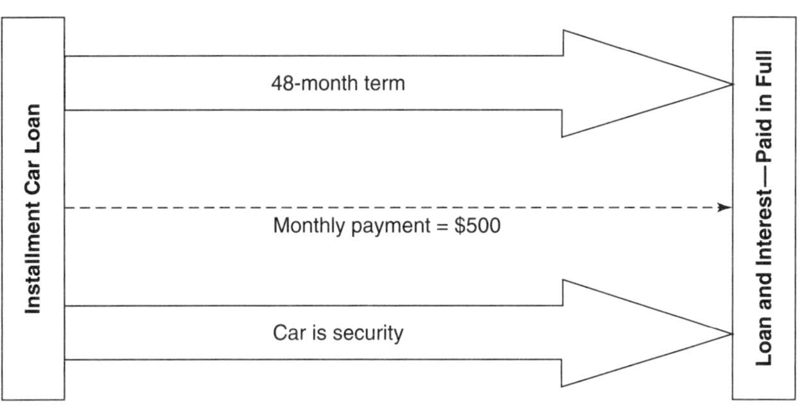

EXHIBIT 1.5

Unsecured Installment Loan

A credit card account is a type of unsecured installment credit. The interest rate and outstanding balance on these types of credit vary so the payments also vary. However, a minimum payment amount is required on a monthly basis.

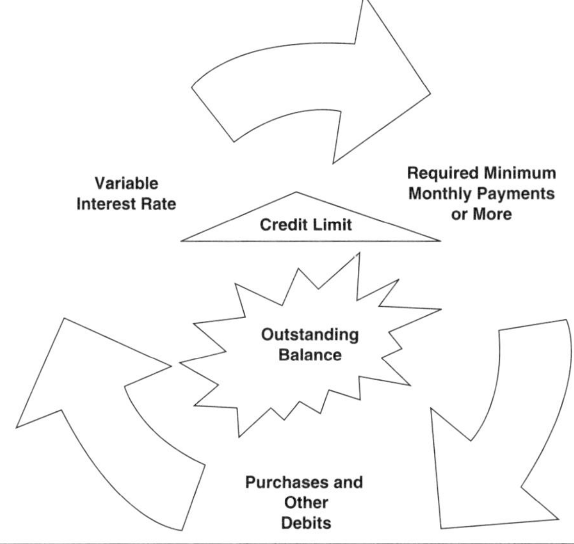

In the Real World

Bob obtained a mortgage loan to purchase his home 20 years ago. Now he wants to remodel the kitchen, so he obtains a home equity loan.

He can borrow additional funds against the security of his home because his equity has increased above the original down payment *and* he has established a good record of making his payments promptly.

The value of Bob's home is $200,000 and the outstanding balance of the mortgage is $70,000.

Remember how to determine Bob's equity?

$200,000 − $70,000 = $130,000

Bob's equity = $130,000

Bob can obtain a home equity loan against the security of his $130,000 home equity.

Home equity loans can be closed or open end. An open-end loan is often referred to as a HELOC (home equity line of credit) and operates like other lines of credit.

Other Products and Services

Banking also includes a great variety of additional products and services that meet customers' financial needs. A few of these products and services are cash management, retirement plans, and safe deposit boxes.

Cash Management

Banking includes many services provided primarily to businesses under the umbrella term of *cash management*. Cash management is a package of banking services that help keep funds working, speed up the payment receipt process, and improve profitability.

A company can use cash management services in these ways as well as others:

- Balances in transaction accounts are kept low and other idle funds are maintained in interest-earning accounts.
- Interest-earning funds are transferred into transaction accounts only when needed to meet checks presented for payment.
- Lockbox services are used so that payments from customers are deposited more quickly to the business's deposit accounts.

A lockbox is a collection system where customers—usually of a business—send payments to a central location for the facilitation of rapid collection. Typically a bank provides the service on behalf of its customers. The bank commonly receives payment and facilitates speedy deposit into the customer's deposit accounts.

Retirement Plans

Another bank deposit vehicle is in the area of retirement plans. Most retirement plans are set up to enable individuals and businesses to save taxes on funds put aside for retirement. Different retirement plans are available, but most allow individuals to defer or reduce taxes on the amounts they save and earn through the plans.

An example of a retirement plan set up by a business for its employees is a *401(k) plan*, named after the section in the Internal Revenue Code that establishes the rules for these plans. Under these plans, employees choose to have their employer contribute a percentage of the employee's income on a pretax basis. The employee defers taxes on the contribution and its earnings until retirement. The employer may also match all or a portion of the employee's contribution to the plan.

Another popular retirement plan is an *individual retirement account* (IRA). Any individual with earned income can establish an IRA and make contributions to it up to a set limit. The earnings on the contributions are tax-deferred or tax-free depending on the type of IRA (many different variations are available). The contributions may or may not be tax-deductible depending on the type of IRA.

Options for investing IRA funds vary. Banks may offer both deposit account options and brokerage accounts (often by way of a brokerage that is a subsidiary or affiliate of the bank). With a brokerage account, the customer can invest in mutual funds, stocks, bonds, and other uninsured investments. Customers make their choice based on their risk tolerance (insured deposit accounts versus uninsured alternative investments), amount being saved, and time horizon for retirement. Most customers need to weigh many considerations when deciding on the type of IRA that is appropriate for them. Depending on their tax situation, they may need to consult a tax expert.

Safe Deposit Boxes

Another banking service that may be available to customers is a safe deposit box. Customers rent metal boxes (various sizes are available) that are stored in a vault in the bank. In these boxes, customers typically store valuable papers and small objects, such as family heirlooms. The boxes have two locks so that unauthorized access is prevented; the customer has one key and the bank has the other.

Check Clearing

Due to the historical popularity and volume of checks used every day, banking devotes significant resources to the processing of check payments. Over the years, the financial system has modernized and improved the check clearing system so that electronic debits and credits speed up the transfer of funds, even though physical checks sometimes are still used. With the passage of the Check Clearing for the 21st Century Act (Check 21) in 2003 (effective October 28, 2004), banks are able to process even more checks electronically, further reducing expenses associated with transporting paper checks.

Under Check 21, a new negotiable instrument called a *substitute check* (a specially formatted paper copy of the front and back of an original check) is allowed, permitting banks to process check information electronically and to deliver substitute checks to any banks that want to continue receiving paper checks. A substitute check is the legal equivalent of the original check and includes all the information contained on the original check. Check 21 does not require banks to accept checks in electronic form nor does it require banks to use the new authority granted by the Act to create substitute checks.

The check-clearing process is more complex than it was in the past because of the volume of transactions involved on a daily basis, not to mention changes in regulations impacting clearing and constantly changing technology. Many banks send their checks to a Federal Reserve Bank (the Fed) for check clearing. The Fed sorts the checks and conducts the process of sending the checks and handling the debits and credits.

As you can imagine, if a check written on a bank in one town is sent to a business in another town, the process becomes slow and inefficient. Until recently, banks have had to send a physical check through various intermediaries before the payment process was complete. Imagine the volume of paper that was shipped around the country for a process like this to work. Even though most checks cleared quickly, the process was still laborious.

Exhibit 1.6 shows a simplistic version of how the check-clearing system works.

Electronic Transactions = Instantaneous Transfers of Funds

While check clearing is still an important payment system, banking has found cheaper and faster ways to transfer funds. Today the banking system processes more and more electronic transactions to make payments and transfer funds.

Electronic transactions allow for instantaneous transfers of funds to almost anywhere in the world. Documentation for transfers does not

EXHIBIT 1.6

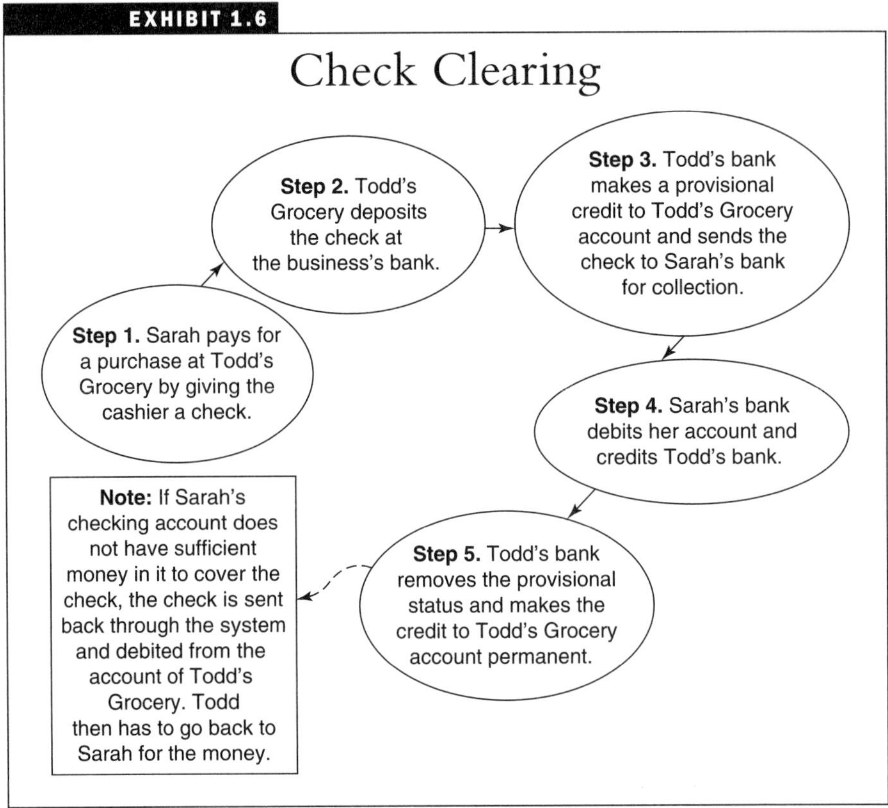

have to be physically carried from one spot to another. Electronic messages supply all the information that is needed to process transfers of funds.

Customers now have access to such a variety of electronic banking services that they can execute most banking transactions remotely. Although many customers still visit bank offices, the use of electronic banking services continues to grow each year. Electronic banking services include remote terminal transactions, telephone transactions, and other electronic transactions such as those conducted via the Internet.

Remote terminals expand the reach of banking offices by allowing customers to make transactions at another location. Remote terminals are simply machines that allow customers to access accounts without the personal assistance of a bank employee.

We'll discuss four types of remote terminal transactions in this chapter:

1. Automated teller machines (ATMs)
2. Point-of-sale terminals (POS)
3. Online access
4. Telephone transactions

ATMs

A popular type of remote terminal is an automated teller machine. ATMs allow customers to conduct a variety of transactions on their accounts, such as withdrawals, deposits, loan and credit card payments, and balance and account history inquiries.

ATMs owned by banking institutions usually allow for a wide range of services. ATMs that are owned by other businesses, such as convenience stores, often are merely cash dispensers that allow only withdrawals.

ATMs have been around for decades, but their technology continues to improve. The newest types of ATMs now allow for Check 21 deposits and nonbanking purchases such as postage stamps, public transit cards, and prepaid telephone cards.

The types of security used to protect customers' accounts from unauthorized transactions on ATMs are also evolving. Currently the most frequent method of providing authorized access to a person's account is through the use of a plastic card and an access code called a *personal identification number* (PIN). The customer either selects the PIN or the card issuer assigns the PIN.

Some machines use biometrics to check identity. Biometrics is a measurement of some physical aspect of a person that can be verified to authorize a transaction. For example, a fingertip scanner can verify the person's fingerprint against a stored record, or an iris scanner checks the person's identity by scanning the iris of the eye.

Point-of-Sale Terminals

Another type of remote terminal is a point-of-sale (POS) terminal. A POS terminal is located at a merchant, and the customer uses the terminal to authorize a transfer of funds from his or her deposit account directly to the merchant's bank account.

To authorize the transaction, the customer presents a debit card, which is similar to an ATM card except that the only transactions that can be authorized are transfers from the account. Some merchants, such as supermarkets, allow customers to use a debit card to pay for merchandise and receive additional cash. Some banks offer cards that combine the functions of an ATM card and debit card.

Online Access

Financial transactions using a personal computer and the Internet are another common type of remote terminal transaction. Financial institutions establish web sites with varying degrees of transaction capability. Some web sites provide information only, such as interest rates and product features, and include an e-mail address for communication. Other information sites offer interactive features, such as on-screen financial calculators, which can help customers calculate the yield on an investment, estimate loan payments, and calculate how much money to save for retirement.

Today most banking web sites offer customers the ability to conduct transactions on their accounts and make inquiries. These programs usually require the customer to use a personal identification number to access his or her accounts. The types of transactions available usually include transfers and payments. Customers also may have the ability to download account information into money management software on their computers. Doing so speeds up account reconciliation and can make tax filing easier.

Customers who regularly use Internet banking services enjoy the convenience of accessing their accounts at any time and from the comfort of their home. They can access their checking account to see if a check has cleared and can schedule bill payments that are deducted from their accounts.

Customers can even fill out loan applications and receive online loan approvals. The approved loan amount can be credited to the customer's checking account.

Telephone Transactions

Most customers can access their accounts using automated telephone banking systems. These systems are also known as audio response systems or interactive voice response (IVR) systems.

Customers call the bank and gain access to their accounts through the use of a PIN password or other identifying information. After the phone system presents a recorded list of menu options, the customer presses a number or speaks a response to proceed. Customers can authorize transfers from their accounts by pressing keys on the phone keypad or speaking a response from a list of menu options. They can also check account balances, find out if checks have cleared, make loan payments, obtain interest information, and check maturity dates on certificate accounts. Some systems also allow customers to apply for a loan.

Other Types of Electronic Transactions

Other types of electronic transactions have been available for decades. While they use electronic communication methods to transfer funds, these systems are not under the direct control of the customer. They are handled completely by the banking system after the customer makes the request. The best-known types of these electronic communication methods are automated clearinghouse (ACH) transactions and wire transfers.

Automated clearinghouses are organizations that electronically send debits and credits between member organizations, typically banks.

EXHIBIT 1.7

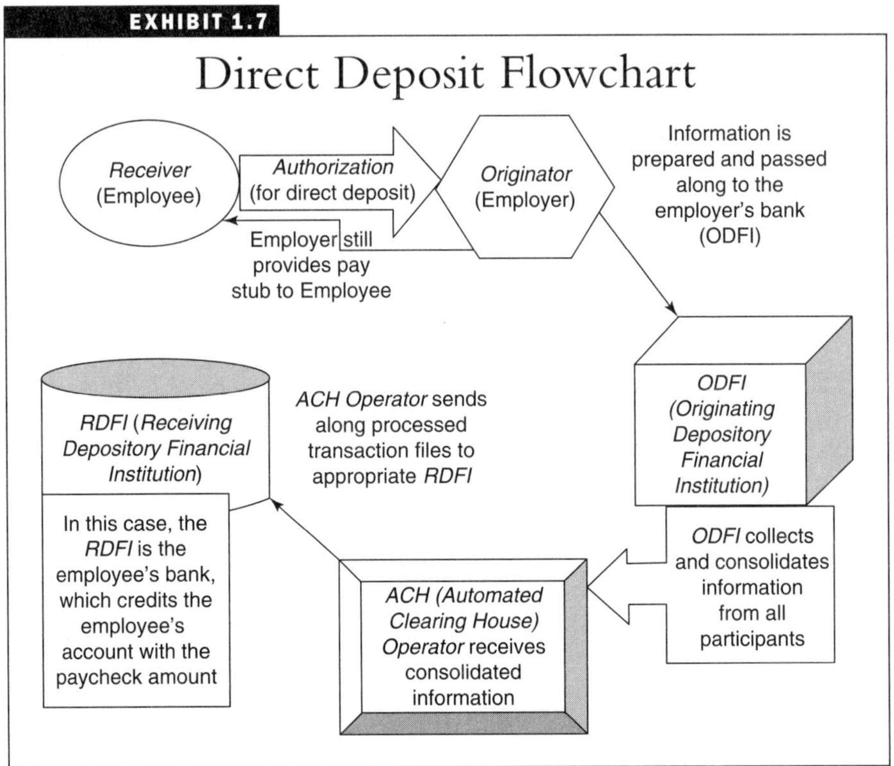

Typical ACH transactions include payment of utility bills, loan payments, and direct deposit of recurring payments, such as social security or payroll.

Exhibit 1.7 is an example of how a payroll direct deposit flows through an ACH system.

Once the customer requests the service and it is set up, most ACH transactions continue until canceled by the customer. ACH transactions are cheaper than check transactions for banks to process, so customers are encouraged to use them. ACH transfers are safer than sending checks through the mail because no physical object must be delivered and transactions can be tracked.

ACH transactions offer great convenience for customers because these transactions need no further maintenance once they are established. Payments and deposits recur automatically.

Wire transfers are another type of electronic banking service that customers may request. A wire transfer is an electronic movement of funds from one banking institution to another. The transfer usually takes place on the same day as it is requested. Wire transfers are a safe and quick way to move funds between banks because checks are not involved in the process.

Summary

The banking industry in the United States traces its roots back to the days of barter—trading without the use of money. While banks existed before money (originally coins) was invented, they became even more important as the notion of financial intermediaries evolved and money was accepted as a superior alternative to barter.

Over time, banks evolved to their current definition as an establishment for the custody, loan, exchange, or issue of money, for the extension of credit, and for facilitating the transmission of funds. Ever since money was first created, banks have been playing an important, if not central, role as financial intermediators.

Banks, as financial intermediators, act as the go-between for individuals and businesses that have extra money and those that wish to borrow money. By accepting funds from one source and using the money to make loans or other investments, banks help create money with each set of transactions. Customers turn to banks for many reasons: to borrow money to achieve goals, to prevent losses, to facilitate returns on idle funds, and to manage funds conveniently and efficiently.

Banks today offer a wealth of products and services including certificates of deposit, money market accounts, retirement plans, commercial loans, cash management, funds transfer services, payment processing, and, of course, checking and savings accounts. Banks also offer variations on these accounts, including holiday club accounts and vacation club accounts.

Most banks also offer business and consumer loans. Business loans include lines of credit, short-term loans, and long-term loans. A short-term loan is usually less than a year and typically used for a seasonal need. Long-term loans are longer than a year and are typically used to expand business or purchase equipment. Payments are typically from business income and paid in installments. Consumer loans are installment loans and mortgage loans. Mortgage loans are loans secured with real estate and typically used to purchase a home. Home equity loans are a second type of real estate loan and secured by the part of the real estate that belongs to the homeowner (the homeowner's equity).

To facilitate these products and services, technology plays a critical and ever-increasing role in our banking system. Online banking, ATMs, sophisticated telephone banking systems, and wireless access and other technology-enabled services help bring more and more complex services to bank customers, faster and more reliably.

CHAPTER 2

Deposit Insurance and the Regulatory Environment: How Does It All Work?

After reading this chapter, you will be able to:

- Understand why banking is a highly regulated business.
- Describe how laws become regulations.
- Discuss how banks are regulated.
- Recognize the primary government agencies that regulate banks.
- Identify which agency is responsible for insured deposits.

Banking is a highly regulated business. The banking regulatory system is the cornerstone of banking in the United States today. This chapter will familiarize you with the regulatory environment and help you to understand how it impacts all aspects of our financial system.

Why Is Regulation Important?

Regulation helps maintain customers' trust in the banking system. Customers have a high level of trust in banking due to the combination of competent banking employees and the "security blanket" of government supervision.

Regulations are a source of many policies and procedures in banks that must be followed as part of the banking business. Procedures that are the result of regulatory requirements must be followed very closely and documented to demonstrate compliance. When a bank implements a procedure that is required by a regulation, exceptions are unlikely.

Banks, unlike many other businesses, are heavily regulated by state and federal governments. This regulation is necessary primarily because of banking's traditional role in the payments system (historically through cash and checks) and in providing credit to businesses and individuals.

For as long as we have had banks, the stability of the nation's economy has been strongly tied to the stability of banking. In the post-Depression era, the federal government became concerned about bank failures and became more and more involved in regulation. The federal government established deposit insurance to protect individuals from losses due to bank failures. To maintain stability in the economy and protect the federal government's guarantee of deposits, it established agencies and regulations that supervise and monitor banking activities.

The government has also taken on the role to protect consumers from discrimination or other unfair practices in financial institutions. To accomplish this goal, the federal government has passed laws that require certain disclosures and other activities. Regulators monitor compliance with these laws.

The U.S. Congress passes laws that create requirements for businesses. For example, the Equal Credit Opportunity Act is a federal law that prohibits lenders from discriminating against credit applicants on the basis of factors such as race, color, sex, marital status, religion, age, or national origin. But when passing a law such as this, Congress must consider how the law will be enforced. Enforcement of laws related to banking often is assigned to regulatory agencies.

Regulatory Agencies

Regulatory agencies are given the authority to interpret the laws and write rules that more specifically carry out the requirements of the laws. To do this, the agencies propose rules and release them for comment. During the comment period, interested citizens and businesses can send their opinions about the proposed rule to the regulatory agency. In addition, the agency may hold hearings where individuals testify and are questioned.

After gathering responses to the proposed rule, the agency issues a final rule or a new proposed rule, or withdraws the proposed rule. A final rule can be the same as the proposed rule, or it can be considerably different. This process allows banking professionals significant input into the rulemaking process and often results in rules that are more reasonable and practical than the original proposal but still achieve the goal of the law.

The regulatory agencies that have the most significant effect on banking are:

- The Board of Governors of the Federal Reserve System (the Fed)
- State regulatory agencies
- Office of the Comptroller of the Currency (OCC)
- Federal Deposit Insurance Corporation (FDIC)

Regulation of the banking business is fragmented among different agencies primarily because of historical differences among various types of financial institutions. Responsibility for banking regulation will continue to shift in the future due to constantly changing laws. It is important, however, to have a general understanding of the regulators' responsibilities and how they affect banking activities.

One of the ways that regulators insure compliance with bank regulations is to conduct bank examinations. Often banks may find that while "the examiners are here," they will see a few strangers around the office. Unless bank employees need to produce records for the examiners or answer questions about their responsibilities, however, the examiners' brief presence may be the only visible sign of government supervision at the bank. Customers will not notice any changes in the bank's services during such an examination. The presence of regulators during the examination period almost never impacts the day-to-day operation of the bank. Banks also conduct internal examinations and audits as part of their own regulatory oversight and to ensure that their employees are in compliance with regulatory requirements.

Federal Reserve System

The Federal Reserve System (commonly referred to as the Fed) is the central bank of the United States. The Federal Reserve System has a network of 12 regional Federal Reserve Banks plus 25 branches. The Fed has several duties that meet its primary responsibility to provide a safe, flexible, and stable monetary and financial system.

- The Fed conducts the nation's monetary policy by influencing the money and credit conditions with the goal of full employment and stable prices.
- The Fed supervises and regulates banking institutions to maintain a safe and sound financial system and protect the financial rights of consumers.
- The Fed provides certain financial services to the U.S. government, financial institutions, and the public, especially in payment system processes.

Each of these responsibilities is explained in this section.

Conduct Monetary Policy

The Federal Reserve System conducts monetary policy using three methods:

1. *Open market operations.* The Fed buys and sells U.S. government securities (such as Treasury bills and notes) in the open market to influence the level of reserves in the depository system.
2. *Reserve requirements.* The Fed sets requirements regarding the amount of funds that banking institutions must hold in reserve against deposits. These funds can be held at the bank or the Fed and cannot be lent out.
3. *Discount rate.* The Fed controls the interest rate (called the discount rate) it charges to banking institutions when they borrow funds from a regional Federal Reserve Bank.

Supervise and Regulate Banking Institutions

Some Federal Reserve regulations apply to the entire banking system; others apply only to banks that are members of the Federal Reserve System. Members include state banks that have chosen to join the Federal Reserve System and national banks, which are automatically members. The Fed also issues regulations to carry out major federal laws regarding consumer protection. Responsibility for supervision of banks is shared with the OCC, FDIC, and state banking regulators. The primary supervision for a bank depends on the charter type of the banking institution. For example, national banks are chartered by the OCC but banks can also be chartered under state law. Banks chartered under state law are supervised by state banking departments.

Provide Reserve Bank Services

The 12 Federal Reserve Banks provide services to banking institutions and the federal government.

For banking institutions, the Federal Reserve Banks provide payment services such as:

- Collecting checks
- Electronically transferring funds
- Distributing and receiving currency and coin

For the federal government, the Fed:

- Pays Treasury checks
- Processes electronic payments (such as direct deposit of social security payments)
- Sells and redeems U.S. government securities (such as EE savings bonds)

Federal Reserve Districts

The United States is divided into 12 Federal Reserve districts. The following list shows the locations of the 12 district banks.

District Number	District Bank Location
1	Boston
2	New York
3	Philadelphia
4	Cleveland
5	Richmond
6	Atlanta
7	Chicago
8	St. Louis
9	Minneapolis
10	Kansas City
11	Dallas
12	San Francisco

State Regulators

Banks can also be chartered under state law. Just as national banks are chartered by the OCC, state banks are chartered by the banking department of each state's government. State banking departments write regulations and supervise their state banks. The FDIC is the insuring agency for insured deposits at state banks.

Office of the Comptroller of the Currency

The Office of the Comptroller of the Currency is responsible for chartering, regulating, and supervising all national banks.

For a national bank to open for business, it must apply for a charter, or license to operate, from the OCC. The OCC issues regulations regarding bank investments, loans, and other activities. The OCC also visits national banks and examines their activities for compliance with federal laws and regulations. To enforce these laws and regulations, the OCC can take actions against banks that restrict their business activities, remove officers, and assess monetary penalties.

Major functions of the OCC include:

- Ensuring the safety and soundness of the national banking system
- Encouraging competition by allowing banks to offer new products and services
- Giving Americans fair and equal access to banking services

Federal Deposit Insurance Corporation

The Federal Deposit Insurance Corporation was created to increase public confidence in the U.S. banking system. The FDIC provides specific coverage limits to people and entities, or depositors, of financial institutions, in the event of a bank failure. The amount of coverage the FDIC provides depositors depends on the rights and capacities in which deposits are held.

Some bank products are covered by FDIC insurance, and some bank products are not. Only bank deposit accounts are insured. Imagine trying to withdraw money from a nearby ATM machine of your bank only to discover that the bank was no longer in business.

Imagine not being able to withdraw any money from that bank again, because the bank had failed.

Imagine losing all of the money you had on deposit at that bank, with no hope of ever recovering it.

Devastating? Absolutely!

There was a time in the United States when this happened to many bank customers. Prior to the creation of the FDIC, customers had no recourse to recover their deposits at failed banks. Today, federal insurance on deposits plays a key part in the public's confidence in the nation's banking system.

The FDIC was created in 1933 along with a series of other important financial regulations to protect individuals from losing money to failed financial institutions.

As a result of the Stock Market Crash of 1929 and the Great Depression that followed, public confidence in large financial institutions diminished. More than 9,000 banks closed between 1929 and March 1933, when President Franklin Delano Roosevelt took office. Many people took money out of banks, fearing that banks would close and their deposits would not be recoverable. It was a time of high inflation, high unemployment (25 percent), and tremendous national uncertainty.

President Roosevelt originally created the FDIC as a temporary regulatory agency under the Banking Act of 1933 to regulate and supervise banks. He also gave FDIC the authority to insure depositors' funds. In an effort to prevent some of the panic resulting from the Crash of 1929, Roosevelt also stripped banks of the authority to loan money on margin for stocks and to sell stocks altogether.

FDIC coverage insured depositors for up to $2,500 in 1934. That same year, nine FDIC-insured banks failed and the first FDIC-insured depositor was paid.

Since the 1930s, insurance coverage has increased over the years to the current level of $100,000. The following table shows the amount of FDIC coverage for investors from 1934 to the present.

Date	FDIC Coverage
1934	$2,500
1950s	$10,000
1960s	$20,000
1970s	$40,000
1980s to present	$100,000

Today, the American public has a great deal of confidence in the safety of their funds that are insured by the FDIC.

FDIC Insurance and Coverage Limits

The basic coverage amount of a depositor is $100,000 per institution, including principal and interest, regardless of citizenship or country of residence.

Under the Federal Deposit Insurance Reform Act of 2005, the term *standard minimum deposit insurance amount* has been created to cover both the $100,000 limit and the higher $250,000 limit on certain retirement plan accounts.

Although most deposits at an insured institution (other than certain retirement accounts) are subject to the $100,000 insurance limit, deposits maintained in different categories of legal ownership are insured separately. As a result, it is possible for a depositor to have more than $100,000 of insurance coverage at one institution. It is important for depositors to understand the rules governing the $100,000 deposit insurance limit. If depositors misunderstand the rules, they could potentially lose deposited funds if the bank fails. Not all bank deposits are insured.

Insured Bank Deposits

- Checking, money market, and demand deposit accounts
- Savings, passbook savings, and Christmas and vacation club accounts

- Certificates of deposit and other time deposits
- NOW (negotiable order of withdrawal) accounts
- Retirement accounts (cash on deposit only, not investments)
- Cashier's checks, money orders, outstanding drafts, and officers' checks
- Certified checks, letters of credit, travelers' checks (insured when issued in exchange for money or a charge against a deposit account)

Uninsured Bank Products

- Mutual funds, including money market mutual funds
- U.S. Treasury bills, notes, and bonds
- Insurance annuities, either fixed or variable
- Stocks, bonds, or other investment securities
- Safe deposit box contents
- Funds lost by the institution as a result of robbery, theft, fraud, embezzlement, or natural disaster (usually covered by the institution's bond insurance)

The In the Real World box shows how FDIC insurance might work in one scenario.

When an Institution Fails

FDIC insurance coverage was created to insure depositors in the event of a bank failure. Banks can fail for any number of reasons:

- An economic downturn substantially decreases the amount of income, and/or the value, of the loans held by the bank.
- The capital reserves of the bank fall below minimum levels as a result of losses on assets and/or bank operations.
- A lending institution is weighed down by bad or fraudulent loans and/or is so poorly operated that it is extremely difficult to determine its true financial condition.

Alan, Brenda, and Caitlin own three joint accounts.

Account	Owners	Balance
Checking	Alan and Brenda	$130,000
Savings #1	Brenda and Alan	$50,000
Savings #2	Alan, Brenda, and Caitlin	$90,000

Here are their ownership interests in each of the accounts.

Alan's Ownership Interest	
1/2 of the balance in Checking:	$65,000
1/2 of the balance of Savings #1:	$25,000
1/3 of the balance in Savings #2:	$30,000
Total of Alan's ownership interests:	$120,000

Alan's insurance coverage is limited to $100,000, so $20,000 of his funds on deposit are not FDIC insured.

Brenda's Ownership Interest

1/2 of the balance in Checking:	$65,000
1/2 of the balance in Savings #1:	$25,000
1/3 of the balance in Savings #2:	$30,000
Total of Brenda's ownership interests:	$120,000

Since Brenda's insurance coverage is $100,000, $20,000 of her funds on deposit are not FDIC insured.

Caitlin's Ownership Interest

1/3 of the balance in Savings #2:	$30,000
Total of Caitlin's ownership interests:	$30,000

In the Real World (continued)

Caitlin's insurance coverage is $100,000, so all of her funds on deposit are FDIC insured.

Insurance Coverage Summary

	Insured	Not Insured
Alan	$100,000	$20,000
Brenda	$100,000	$20,000
Caitlin	$30,000	
Total	$230,000	$40,000

Regulatory Reaction to Bank Failures

Banks are regulated and supervised by the Federal Reserve, the Office of the Comptroller of the Currency (OCC), the FDIC, and/or state banking authorities where the bank is headquartered. Savings and loans are regulated and supervised by the Office of Thrift Supervision (OTS) or by state authorities.

The FDIC is the only governmental agency that insures the deposits in an insured bank or savings and loan. Typically, through its ongoing monitoring activities, the bank's supervisor will begin to take special notice of banks that appear to be headed toward default and will notify the FDIC.

The FDIC is responsible for seeing that depositors will be paid the insured amount of their deposit account(s) and for selling the assets of the failed bank. The FDIC also investigates the cause(s) of the bank's failure and will refer any evidence of criminal activity to the proper legal authorities.

Once an institution is near default, the FDIC deploys an extensive team of bank liquidation professionals who are tasked with investigating the failed institution and determining how to manage the liquidation. Often the insolvent bank is sold to a solvent bank, and the bank reopens within days under the new bank name.

Unfortunately, as news of the possible bank failure spreads throughout the bank's community, many depositors withdraw all of their funds at the bank, further deepening the damage to the bank. In an effort to stem the problem, the FDIC investigates and liquidates banks quietly, making every ethical effort to quell panic and to quickly resolve the situation.

Protection of Depositors

The bank's regulator makes every effort to prevent banks from failing. The regulator monitors banks regularly and can mandate corrective-action orders to a bank to resolve problems that could lead to failure.

In addition, a majority of the five-member FDIC board can vote to exercise a backup exam authority in which FDIC officials investigate the activities of a bank.

Action orders can include mandating that a bank sell voting shares or obligations to become adequately capitalized or forbidding the bank from lending until its capital has risen to acceptable levels. The FDIC risk-based capital ratio minimum is 8 percent. If an institution falls below this, the FDIC can prohibit the bank from further lending.

If the bank still fails to gain adequate capital, the FDIC takes immediate action. It is critical that financial institution representatives thoroughly understand all of the FDIC insurance deposit scenarios described in this book, because often depositors discover whether their deposits are insured only when the institution. Whether through poor judgment, bad luck, or criminal behavior, some banks do fail.

Deposits Moved to Another FDIC-Insured Institution

In most cases, the FDIC will make arrangements for another FDIC-insured institution to take the insured deposits of the failed institution. Typically, depositors will have access to their insured funds on the next regular business day. If the depositor already has funds at the new institution, his or her deposits are insured separately from those of the failed institution for a set period of time, usually six months or until certificate of deposit (CD) accounts mature.

The new institution may choose to lower interest rates after notifying depositors, and depositors may withdraw funds in CDs without paying an early withdrawal penalty.

Direct Payments to Depositors

If the FDIC is unable to arrange for another insured institution to take on the failed institution's deposits, the FDIC pays insurance directly to each depositor.

Summary

One of the unique characteristics of banking, compared to other businesses, is the fact that state and federal governments heavily regulate banks. The amount of regulation is primarily because of banking's traditional role in the payments system (historically through cash and checks) and in providing credit to businesses and individuals.

For as long as we have had banks, the stability of the nation's economy has been strongly tied to the stability of banking. Going back to the post-Depression era, when the federal government became concerned about bank failures, government became more and more involved in regulation. To maintain stability in the economy and protect its guarantee of deposits, the federal government established agencies and regulations that supervise and monitor banking activities.

The government has also taken on the role of protecting consumers from discrimination or other unfair practices in financial institutions. To accomplish this goal, the federal government has passed laws that require certain disclosures and other activities. Regulators monitor compliance with these laws.

Summary

Regulatory agencies are given the authority to interpret the laws and write rules that more specifically carry out the requirements of the laws. To do this, the agencies propose rules and release them for comment. During the comment period, interested citizens and businesses can send their opinions about the proposed rule to the regulatory agency. Additionally, the agency may hold hearings where individuals testify and are questioned.

After gathering responses to the proposed rule, the agency issues a final rule, a new proposed rule, or withdraws the proposed rule. A final rule can be the same as the proposed rule, or it can be considerably different. The process of gathering responses to a proposed change through a comment period or holding hearings, before instituting a rule change, allows for significant input by banking professionals into the rulemaking process and often results in rules that are more reasonable and practical than the original proposal but still achieve the goal of the law.

One of the ways that regulators insure compliance with bank regulations is by conducting bank examinations. The presence of regulators almost never impacts the bank's day-to-day operation during the examination period. Banks also conduct internal examinations and audits as part of their own regulatory oversight and to ensure that their employees are in compliance with regulatory requirements.

The regulators that have the most significant effect on banking are the Board of Governors of the Federal Reserve System, state regulatory agencies, the Office of the Comptroller of the Currency, and the Federal Deposit Insurance Corporation.

CHAPTER 3

Understanding Banking Deposit Accounts, Interest Rates, and Limitations

After reading this chapter, you will be able to:

- Explain the role of government-regulated interest rates in bank competition.
- Identify two major categories of accounts.
- Explain the purpose of demand deposit accounts.
- Discuss the major characteristics of deposit accounts

Many banks have a rate board in their lobby that lists the interest paid on various kinds of accounts. A lot goes into setting the numbers that you see on the board.

In this chapter we'll take a behind-the-scenes look at the rate-setting process. After reading it, you may never look at a rate board the same way again.

While economic and competitive factors influence both the types of accounts offered by banks and the interest they pay, federal government regulations designed to protect our financial system also play a part in these decisions.

Protecting Our Financial System

While less restricted than in the past, banks are still limited in the accounts they can offer, and consumers are limited in how they can use those accounts. The original interest in deposits regulations came about as a result of the Great Depression of the 1930s, when many depositors lost money because banks failed. In the aftermath of these bank failures, the federal government enacted a number of laws designed to prevent future problems. An example of this is Regulation D (Reg D), which set requirements on the amount financial institutions had to keep in reserve in order to take in deposits and make loans.

Another regulation, Regulation Q (Reg Q), was written to regulate interest on deposits and to address the lack of interest rate uniformity that led to problems during the Depression. Due to this regulation, consumers could make educated decisions about where to invest, because banks had to list and advertise interest rates in a uniform manner. From the 1930s to the late 1970s, the government regulated the interest rates financial institutions could pay on deposits.

Interest rate ceilings kept rates on deposits low, and there was little competition for these deposits. However, in the late 1970s and early 1980s, nonbanks (such as mutual fund companies and securities firms) began to win deposits away from banks. These nonbanks could offer higher interest rates on money market accounts and other investment-driven products because they were not limited by Reg Q and Reg D and

EXHIBIT 3.1

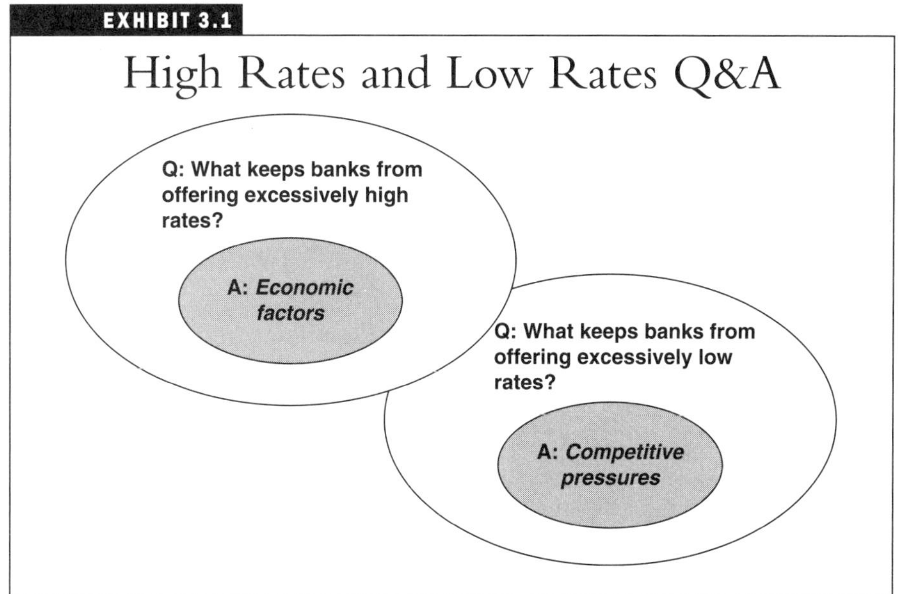

were not federally insured. Bankers asked that the Depression-era rules be changed so that they could compete with these nonbank institutions for customer investments and deposits.

Congress eventually passed the Depository Institutions Deregulation Act of 1980, which eliminated all federal interest rate ceilings on deposit accounts.

In 1986, the last remaining interest rate ceilings were removed, and the deregulation of interest on deposits was complete. Today banks may pay whatever rates they choose on most accounts. Exhibit 3.1 illustrates the questions bankers must answer: Why must rates be neither too high nor too low? It is because the rates must make economic sense to the bank, yet be attractive to customers compared to the bank's competitors.

A few remaining regulations impact interest on deposits, but the regulations don't set rate ceilings. The regulations do define the types of accounts that may be offered and restrictions that affect those accounts.

While banks can pay whatever rates they want, banks cannot pay interest on all types of accounts. In addition, banks must restrict transactions in certain accounts due to reserve requirements.

Basically, reserve requirements maintain that banks cannot lend out or invest all of the money that customers deposit. Banks must keep a certain amount of money in the Federal Reserve System to meet possible withdrawal requests from customers.

The exact amount that must be kept on hand depends on the:

- Amount of money on deposit
- Type of account that money is in

Account Categories

There are two major categories of deposit accounts: transaction accounts and savings accounts.

Transaction Accounts

Transaction accounts are accounts established for the convenience of the account holder. Funds in a transaction account are convenient because they can be accessed without notice to the bank or withdrawn at any time without penalty. A basic checking account (a demand deposit account [DDA]) set up by a customer for the purpose of paying frequent bills and expenses would be an example of this type of transaction account.

Demand Deposit Accounts. Most basic checking accounts that do not pay interest are demand deposit accounts. Account holders typically use basic checking accounts for frequent check writing and automatic electronic payments. A majority of banks offer at least one basic checking account.

DDA Details	Who Uses DDAs?	Who Doesn't Use DDAs?
DDAs have few restrictions on how they can be used. DDA funds can be withdrawn at any time without notice to the bank. DDAs do not pay interest.	Account holders seeking convenience Account holders needing immediate access to their funds.	Account holders seeking interest on their account balances

Interest-paying checking accounts are not considered DDAs.

No interest is paid on demand deposit account balances.

Why?	The accounts generally experience a lot of transactions, which are expensive for banks to process. Paying interest would make the accounts prohibitively expensive for most banks. Consumers can't have everything. (In economics, this truism is known as opportunity cost; there is an opportunity cost to every economic decision we make.) If consumers want the convenience of unlimited transactions, they can't expect to earn interest.

Most DDAs are unprofitable for banks because of the high transaction costs. However, it's widely believed that DDAs are valuable to banks because consumers are likely to do most of their business with the financial institution where they have checking accounts.

Demand deposit accounts do not have a withdrawal advance notice requirement. In addition, there is no maturity period required before funds can be withdrawn. Demand deposit accounts are payable on demand. This means that customers may withdraw money at any time with no advance notice.

In spite of this, banks are legally allowed to have a withdrawal advance notice in place as long as it is less than seven days. However, virtually no banks require this advance notice.

Money can be withdrawn in person, over the phone, by ATM, by mail, over the Internet, or by other methods. Additionally, there are no limitations on the number of withdrawals or transfers that a customer may make into or out of the account.

Because checks are expensive to process, some banks choose to charge a fee to process more than a certain number of checks per month.

Any person or organization may open a demand deposit account, including individual persons or corporations, however, at most banks, business checking accounts have different restrictions from consumer checking accounts.

While DDAs do not pay interest and have no limits on withdrawals or transfers, other account types pay interest and do have limits. If a holder of one of these types of accounts regularly exceeds its limits, the bank can reclassify that account as a demand deposit account. The bank may then stop paying interest on the balance. Bank regulators monitor banks to ensure that they are not giving favorable treatment to some customers by allowing them to earn interest while exceeding the transaction restrictions on interest-earning savings accounts.

NOW Accounts. Negotiable orders of withdrawal accounts are almost always abbreviated as *NOW* accounts. Today few banks actually call these accounts NOW accounts. Instead, they are frequently known as *interest checking* or *gold checking*.

Many banks offer:

- One demand deposit checking account that pays no interest.
- One or more NOW checking accounts that do pay interest.

There are typically more restrictions on NOW accounts than on demand deposit checking. Such restrictions may include a minimum balance that must be maintained or a limit on the number of checks that may be written per month (or both).

The interest rate on NOW accounts is usually relatively low when compared to savings accounts.

There is no maturity period required before funds may be withdrawn from NOW accounts. That means that account holders can take money out at any time. However, some banks have individual policies that require withdrawals to be of a minimum size. And, as mentioned, banks may restrict the number of withdrawals per month. The idea is to lower the average number of monthly transactions, thereby lowering the bank's monthly processing costs. This helps to offset the cost of paying interest on NOW accounts.

Not all banks impose transaction limits on NOW accounts. Much depends on local market pressures and the demographics of the customer base.

As for DDA accounts, banks are legally allowed to have a seven-day withdrawal advance notice in place, but there are virtually no banks that require this advance notice.

NOW accounts may be held only by individuals, government units, or nonprofit organizations. Funds may be accessed by check, draft, telephone, or electronic order or instruction to pay third parties or make payments to another of the depositor's accounts at the same institution.

Super NOW accounts are NOW accounts that:

- Require a minimum balance and pay a higher interest rate
- Have no federally imposed transaction limits, although the bank may impose limits
- May pay any rate of interest

Banks usually require that account balances stay above a certain level in order for account holders to collect the interest rate.

For example, a bank might offer . . .

- A NOW account that pays 4.0 percent interest and has a $500 opening deposit requirement and a $500 minimum balance that must be maintained.
- A Super NOW account that pays 5.0 percent interest and has a $5,000 opening deposit requirement and a $2,500 minimum balance that must be maintained.

Corporations are not allowed to open/hold NOW accounts. Of course, this doesn't mean that corporations cannot have checking accounts. It simply means that most businesses do not earn interest on their business checking accounts because they are limited to demand deposit accounts.

Banks typically offer separate business checking accounts (for corporations). The rules and restrictions on these accounts are far more complex than those for consumer accounts.

Savings Accounts

Savings accounts are used primarily to save money for the (relatively) long term and earn interest on that money. These accounts have more restrictions on how they can be used and how frequently transactions can be conducted. Examples of savings accounts are time deposit accounts (such as certificates of Deposit [CDs]) and savings deposit accounts (such as basic savings).

Savings Deposit Accounts. Savings deposit accounts are considered part of the savings category. These are the basic savings accounts that banks offer to customers these accounts are used primarily to save money and earn interest, and are restrictive in the transactions allowed. Because money may be withdrawn at any time, the interest earned is typically lower than for more restrictive types of savings accounts.

> Savings deposit accounts pay interest on account balances, but they do not have a maturity period. Although most banks pay interest quarterly, interest may be paid daily, weekly, quarterly, or any other set term.

Banks must disclose how they pay interest to new account holders and must adhere to this schedule.

Because the account holder is not agreeing to leave the money in the account for a set amount of time, savings deposit accounts usually pay a lower rate of interest than accounts with time requirements, such as CDs.

For example:

- A savings deposit account might pay 4 percent at a bank.
- A one-year CD might pay 6 percent.

The difference is due to the fact that the bank cannot plan to have the money in the savings account for one year. This reduces the value of the money on deposit to the bank.

Savings account holders are limited to six transfers and six withdrawals per month. These limits are in place because banks must meet reserve requirements:

Reserve Requirements	
$ in checking accounts	Banks must keep a higher percentage of cash on hand relative to deposits because of the transaction nature of these accounts.
$ in savings accounts	Banks can keep a lower percentage of money on hand relative to deposits because these savings accounts are primarily established for earning interest

Account holders are limited in the number of withdrawals and transfers in order to:

- Keep processing costs lower.
- Protect banks from not having enough money on hand.

No more than three of the six allowable transfers per month may be made by:

- Check
- Draft

- Debit card
- Similar order payable to third parties

This requirement is in place to make sure that savings accounts are not used as a substitute for checking accounts.

For example: An account holder may have a cashier's check drawn out of savings to pay a mortgage down payment. However, that same account holder would need to use a checking account to make regularly occurring payments that exceeded the limit of three checks.

However, unlimited transfers are allowed:

- By mail
- By messenger
- By ATM
- In person
- By phone

All types of savings accounts must reserve the right to advance withdrawal notice. Banks must reserve the right to require at least seven days' notice of an account holder's plans to withdraw funds from a savings account (often called the seven-day notice period). For example, if Sara wants to take $500 out of her savings account on January 7, technically, she would need to let the bank know of withdrawal intent by January 1.

Since the right to advance withdrawal notice was first established in 1935, no bank has ever enforced this requirement because of competitive pressures. However, the notice was originally included in the law to prevent the type of bank runs that occurred during the Depression of the 1930s.

Money Market Deposit Accounts. The Bank Rate Monitor web site (www.bankrate.com) describes money market deposit accounts as combining "the liquidity of ready cash with the knuckle-rapping discipline imposed by a federal limit on certain transactions."

Money market deposit accounts (MMDAs) are savings accounts that give the account holder access to funds through:

- Checks
- Drafts
- Debit cards
- Similar financial instruments

These accounts are popular with customers who want a somewhat higher interest rate but still need the safety of federally insured investments.

Banks were formerly required by federal law to have minimum balances in place for MMDAs, but this requirement was repealed. However, most banks still require a minimum balance to open or maintain an MMDA. As a result, MMDAs:

- Are more popular with higher-income consumers who are relatively sophisticated in managing their money
- Almost always require an opening deposit of at least $500

MMDAs are popular because funds are readily available and federally insured. They also earn a higher-than-average interest rate, which also makes them attractive. Like other savings accounts, MMDAs limit account holder withdrawals or transfers to six per month with more than three transfers by check, draft, debit card, or similar orders. These restrictions are why MMDAs fall into the savings accounts category rather than transaction accounts. Remember, transfer limits do not apply to transfers made by mail, messenger, or ATM, in person, or by telephone.

Some banks promote the (limited) check-writing access that MMDAs offer as an added benefit. Account holders who need a traditional checking account and will write a large quantity of checks should not open an MMDA for this purpose.

MMDAs pay interest on account balances. The interest rate paid by MMDAs is usually higher than for ordinary savings accounts to compensate for:

- Higher initial deposit
- Minimum balance requirements

For example, a bank might pay 3 percent on a basic savings account and 4.5 percent on an MMDA. The bank would be able to offset the higher interest rate costs because the MMDA has a higher minimum balance:

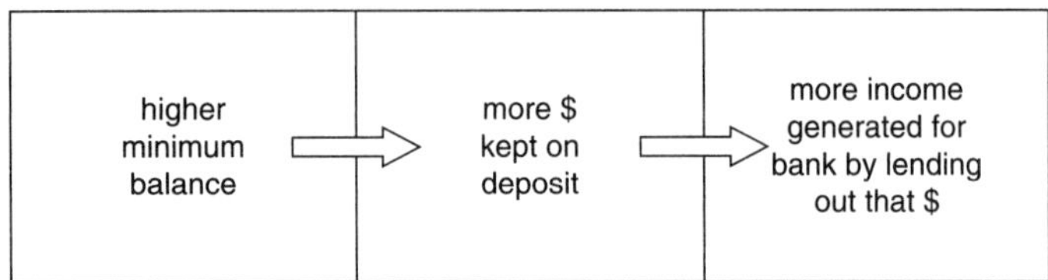

There are no eligibility requirements for MMDAs. MMDAs, however, are typically offered to consumers rather than businesses. In fact, many banks do not allow corporations to open MMDAs.

Some banks and other financial institutions offer three different types of MMDAs, as shown in the table below.

Basic MMDA	**Tiered MMDA**	**Package Deal**
Usually demands a relatively low opening deposit. Pays a lower interest rate.	Usually demands a larger minimum opening deposit than basic accounts. Rewards with a more substantial yield as deposits grow.	Money market account combined with CDs, savings, and other financial investments. Banks sometimes offer a slightly more substantial yield to owners of package deals than to owners of the other two MMDAs. Package deal status may result in a waived minimum deposit.

Time deposit accounts have a set maturity after the date of deposit.	
If funds are withdrawn before this date . . .	The account holder is subject to an early withdrawal financial penalty.
If funds are kept in the account until the agreed-on date . . .	The account holder receives the principal plus the promised rate of interest.

Time Deposit Accounts. Common types of time deposit accounts are:

- Certificates of deposit
- Club accounts (such as holiday club or vacation club)
- Passbook savings

While many banks still offer club accounts, the most common type of time deposit account is the certificate of deposit (CD).

Time deposit accounts always have a maturity of at least seven days from the date of deposit. The exact maturity date is always disclosed in advance and agreed to by both parties. Interest is paid on the deposit balance after the maturity date or when specified in the account contract.

If the deposit is automatically renewable, this fact must be clearly marked on the written contract along with the terms of renewal. Many account holders automatically renew their CDs when they reach maturity because they do not yet need the money on deposit.

As with all savings accounts, banks must reserve the right to receive advance withdrawal notice.

Certificates of Deposit. Common types of time deposit accounts are certificates of deposit (CDs). These accounts feature a contract stating that the account holder will keep funds on deposit for a certain time period. In exchange, the bank agrees to pay a guaranteed rate of interest at the end of that time period. Most banks offer a range of CDs at different terms and requiring different minimum deposits.

Here's an example: Clara, an account holder, takes out a one-year CD on June 1 at a rate of 3.0 percent. Clara must deposit at least $500 in the CD and agrees not to withdraw the funds until one year has passed.

On May 1 of the next year, the bank sends out a notice that Clara's CD will reach maturity in 30 days. The notice states that Clara can withdraw the funds at that time or automatically renew the CD for another year at a certain interest rate.

Clara has two options. She can:

1. *Take no action.* If Clara takes no action by the maturity date of June 1, the CD will automatically be renewed for another year at the current one-year CD interest rate.
2. *Withdraw the funds.* Clara can tell the bank that the funds should be transferred into her savings account on the maturity date. Clara will then be free to withdraw the funds.

Club Accounts. Club accounts are frequently set up to save a certain amount of money for a special occasion (such as a holiday or summer vacation). Club accounts are conducted under a written contract that does not allow withdrawal of funds until a certain number of deposits have been made during a period of at least three months.

For example: Jane, an account holder, establishes a club account to save money for the holidays. Starting in January, she agrees to have $25 automatically transferred each month from her checking account into the holiday club account. In December, Jane has $300 ($25 × 12 months) plus interest saved in her account. Jane can either withdraw that money or keep saving.

Other types of time deposit accounts are:

- Instrument
- Passbook

- Statement
- Book entry notation

Although these accounts are not as popular as they were in the past, they are still offered by some banks. Banks must provide account holders with written statements outlining contractual responsibilities of both parties. Responsibilities include:

- How long the money must be kept on deposit
- How much interest will be paid

All early withdrawal penalties must be disclosed in this contract. Because account holders are agreeing to leave funds on deposit for a certain time period, written disclosures are even more important than for other account types.

In addition to written materials, bankers need to verbally explain the:

- Restrictions on the account
- Penalties that will result if funds are withdrawn early

A combination of written and verbal disclosures will help keep customers well informed and satisfied with the bank.

The presence of an early withdrawal penalty is a key element of time deposit accounts.

When is the early withdrawal penalty imposed?	Who imposes it?
When an account holder withdraws money before the date of maturity	Federal laws impose minimum penalties, but most banks choose to impose further restrictions to avoid early withdrawals

There are federal restrictions on all time deposit accounts.

Early Withdrawal Penalty	No Federally Required Interest Penalty
Equals the loss of 7 days' interest on funds withdrawn within the first 6 days of deposit or within 6 days of a previous partial withdrawal	For funds withdrawn after the first 6 days and not within 6 days of a previous partial withdrawal

However, many banks choose to institute their own more stringent penalties, as shown in the following table:

Situation	Dilemma	Outcome
Mark agrees to a 30-day maturity period on a CD. After 15 days, Mark asks to withdraw the money. There is no federal restriction because it is after the first 6 days. Therefore, the bank is not required to impose a penalty and could legally pay Mark his principal plus the full interest.	However, this is not in the best interest of the bank, because the bank is managing its funds based on the assumption that all time deposits will be untouched until the maturity date. It loans out and invests funds deposited by customers based on this assumption.	Therefore, the bank imposes its own early withdrawal penalty of the loss of 15 days' interest. Mark receives his principal back but does not earn any interest.

Banks cannot impose different penalties for different account holders. They must set a policy and enforce that policy consistently for all account holders.

Nonpersonal Accounts

A nonpersonal account is an account that is held by an organization such as a corporation or other entity rather than individuals. There are a number of complexities with regard to nonpersonal accounts and penalties that are beyond the scope of this book. Please refer to Regulation D for extensive information on this topic.

Computing Interest

Banks use several different methods to compute the interest they pay on deposits. Methods vary by:

- Area of the country
- Size of institution
- Competitive pressures
- A variety of other factors

These methods of computing interest vary widely, and can result in large differences in the amount of interest earned by an account holder.

Interest is paid on the amount of money in the account, so how banks determine that account balance plays a large role in how much interest will be paid.

We'll look at four basic methods for determining the account balance on which interest is paid:

1. Low balance
2. First in, first out (FIFO)
3. Last in, first out (LIFO)
4. Day of deposit to day of withdrawal

Low Balance Method

Under the low balance method, the account holder receives interest on the lowest balance during the quarter. In most situations, the low balance method is the worst for account holders.

First In, First Out Method

Under the FIFO method, each withdrawal is deducted from the balance at the beginning of the quarter and from later deposits if the balance is insufficient.

Day of Deposit to Day of Withdrawal Method

This method is also known as the daily interest method. Interest is earned on the exact amount in the account each day. In most situations, the day of deposit to day of withdrawal method produces the largest amount of interest earned by borrowers.

Summary

As a result of the Great Depression of the 1930s, many depositors lost money when banks failed. To prevent future problems, regulations governing interest on deposits were enacted. Under these regulations, banks had to be uniform in how they listed and advertised interest rates. Finally consumers had a way to make an educated decision. Until the 1970s; banks were also regulated in the interest rates they could pay on deposits. Over time, the regulations have become less restrictive, but they still limit what accounts banks can offer and how consumers can use accounts.

Regulations also set reserve requirements for financial institutions. These reserve requirements must be met in order for banks to take in deposits and make loans. Other regulations were written to regulate interest on deposits and to address the lack of interest rate uniformity.

Congress eventually passed the Depository Institutions Deregulation Act of 1980, which eliminated all federal interest rate ceilings on deposit accounts. In 1986, the last remaining interest rate ceilings were removed and the deregulation of interest on deposits was complete. Today banks may pay whatever rates they choose on most accounts.

A few remaining regulations impact interest on deposits. These regulations do not set rate ceilings but rather define the types of accounts that may be offered and set restrictions that affect those accounts. Restrictions include the types of accounts that can offer interest and limitations on transactions in certain accounts due to reserve requirements. There are two major categories of deposit accounts, transaction accounts and savings accounts.

Summary

Transaction accounts are convenient and less restrictive than savings accounts. Examples of transaction accounts include basic checking accounts (demand deposit accounts) that do not pay interest and NOW (negotiable orders of withdrawal) accounts, which do pay interest on account balances. The term "NOW account" is rarely used today. Such accounts are most commonly known as interest checking, gold checking, and the like.

Account holders use various savings accounts to save money for a longer term and earn interest. These accounts are more restrictive in terms and transactions than DDA and NOW accounts. Certificates of deposit (CDs and time deposit accounts) and basic savings (savings deposit accounts) are examples of these types of accounts.

Banks use several different methods to compute the interest they pay on deposits, including low balance; first in, first out; last in, last out; and day of deposit to day of withdrawal. The method selected depends on a number of factors, including geographical location, the bank's size, and competitive pressures. These methods of computing interest vary widely and can result in large differences in the amount of interest earned by an account holder.

CHAPTER 4

Regulatory Compliance: The Essentials

After reading this chapter, you will be able to:

- Understand the Expedited Funds Availability and Check 21 Acts.
- Explain the Truth in Savings Act.
- Discuss the Electronic Fund Transfer Act.
- Define the Equal Credit Opportunity Act.
- Describe the Truth in Lending Act.
- Demonstrate Understanding of the Bank Privacy Regulations.

Important Consumer Protection Laws

One responsibility of banking regulators is to monitor compliance with consumer protection laws. The Board of Governors of the Federal Reserve System issues the regulations required by many of these laws. This chapter covers consumer protection regulations that are most likely to be encountered in banking. It is not meant to be an extensive guide to these regulations but an overview of important regulations.

The Expedited Funds Availability Act

The Expedited Funds Availability Act (EFAA) was enacted to speed up the collection of checks and other items deposited to transaction accounts and to set time limits on making funds available to consumers. *Regulation CC* (Reg CC), issued by the Board of Governors of the Federal Reserve System, implements EFAA.

When Deposited Items Must Be Available to Consumers

Regulation CC establishes the number of business days within which the funds from different types of deposited items must be made available to consumers. For example, the funds from checks drawn on local banks are required to be made available more quickly than funds from checks drawn on nonlocal banks.

Check Endorsements

Regulation CC also establishes where endorsements should be located on the back of checks. For example, the payee of the check must sign within a certain part of the back of the check. The bank that accepts the deposited check places its endorsement in a separate place on the back of the check. Subsequent endorsements are placed in a third area.

By separating where these endorsements appear, if the check must be returned to the original bank, the process is accomplished more quickly and with fewer errors.

Disclosures to Customers

Bankers encounter the requirements of Regulation CC when they open new transaction accounts for customers. The regulation requires that customers receive a written disclosure of the time limits for availability of the different types of deposited items.

Accepting Checks for Deposit

When accepting checks for deposit, the bank must take actions that comply with Regulation CC. The bank must, for example, make sure that the customer endorses the check in the proper location. And bankers should explain to customers when their funds will be available to them.

Check Clearing for the 21st Century Act

The Check Clearing for the 21st Century Act (Check 21) was signed into law 10/28/2003 (effective 10/28/2004). Check 21 authorizes the use of "substitute checks" as legal equivalents of original checks. Specific requirements must be met for a check to qualify as a "substitute check" Check 21 was created to bring increased efficiency and innovation to our nation's check processing systems. Like EFAA, Check 21 is implemented under Regulation CC.

Requirements for Substitute Checks

Check 21 defines the "substitute check" and the requirements it must meet to qualify as the legal equivalent of the original check. It also addresses the bank's duties and responsibilities and the required disclosures for substitute checks.

To be considered a legal equivalent, the substitute check must:

- Accurately replicate all the information on the original check (front and back)
- Display the legend "This is a legal copy of your check. You can use it the same way you would use the original check."[1]

[1]Occ.treas.gov web site as cited in the Act.

Reg CC Endorsements, Warranties, and Disclosures

A reconverting bank, meaning the bank that creates the substitute check, must also meet Reg CC's standards regarding endorsements described earlier. And any bank that transfers, presents, or returns a substitute check for consideration must warrant that the substitute is a legal equivalent and that a check that has already been paid will not be presented for a second payment.

Additionally banks must follow all other requirements under Reg CC including disclosure and indemnity requirements.

Truth in Savings (Regulation DD)

The Truth in Savings Act was enacted to help consumers make informed decisions about deposit accounts at banking institutions. *Regulation DD* implements the Truth in Savings Act.

Regulation DD requires that consumers receive disclosures of information such as:

- Balance requirements
- Interest rates
- Penalties (if any) and what fees they may incur

The purpose of these disclosures is to allow consumers to make meaningful comparisons among banking institutions.

Customer Inquiries Regarding Interest Rates

Regulation DD may affect your job if you are a banker responsible for opening new accounts or responding to customers' questions about interest rates. When consumers open deposit accounts, the banker is required to give them a written disclosure. Bankers must also give consumers this disclosure if they request one, even if they are not opening an account.

Rate Information

If a consumer asks about interest rates on accounts, rate information must be provided in a specific way. Deposit account rates must be displayed in terms of the annual percentage yield (APY). This is an annual percentage rate that reflects total interest earned including the effects of compounding. An account is considered to earn compounded interest when the credited interest earns interest. The interest rate may also be quoted without compounding, but bankers are always required to quote the APY.

Electronic Fund Transfer (Regulation E)

The Electronic Fund Transfer Act was enacted to establish the basic rights, liabilities, and responsibilities of consumers who use electronic fund transfer services and of financial institutions that offer these services. *Regulation E* implements the Electronic Fund Transfer Act and provides protection of individual consumers engaging in electronic fund transfers.

Examples of electronic fund transfer services include:

- ATM transactions
- Direct deposit of payroll
- Debit card transactions
- Internet banking transfers

Required Disclosures

Under the Electronic Fund Transfer Act, Regulation E requires that customers receive disclosures of information such as:

- Any fees involved in electronic fund transfers
- How to report errors
- How reported errors are investigated and resolved

- Documentation of transactions
- Liability of the customer in case of unauthorized fund transfers (such as fraudulent transactions)

Investigating Errors

Another requirement under Regulation E is that reported errors in electronic transfers must meet certain deadlines for making the investigation, communicating with customers, and resolving the situation.

Equal Credit Opportunity (Regulation B)

The purpose of the Equal Credit Opportunity Act is to promote the availability of credit to all creditworthy applicants without regard to:

- Race
- Color
- Religion
- National origin
- Sex
- Marital status
- Age
- All or part of an applicant's income coming from a public assistance program
- The fact that an applicant has exercised any right under the Consumer Credit Protection Act

Regulation B implements the Equal Credit Opportunity Act and requires creditors to take these actions:

- Notify applicants of action taken on their applications.
- Report credit history in the names of both spouses on an account.
- Retain records of credit applications.

- Collect information about the applicant's race and other personal characteristics in applications for certain housing-related loans.
- Provide applicants with copies of appraisal reports used in connection with credit transactions.

Regulation B requires that loan applicants be treated equally and receive objective consideration of their loan request. The factors in granting a loan are based only on the credit qualifications of the applicant and any asset used for secured loans.

The requirement that all loan applicants be treated fairly also extends to potential loan applicants. It is the banker's responsibility to avoid giving any opinion to potential applicants on whether they are qualified for a loan, thus ensuring fair treatment to all potential applicants.

Truth in Lending (Regulation Z)

The purpose of the Truth in Lending Act is to promote the informed use of consumer credit by requiring disclosures about its terms and cost. *Regulation Z* implements the Truth in Lending Act.

Applicants for certain types of consumer credit must be given a written disclosure on the cost of the loan or other credit. The regulation places certain restrictions on the terms of home loans and regulates certain credit card practices. It also provides a method for fair and prompt resolution of credit billing disputes.

Gramm-Leach-Bliley Act of 1999

The Gramm-Leach-Bliley Act (GLBA) established the framework for the restructuring of the financial services industry and how the regulators supervise it. The long-term result is expected to be greater consolidation of formerly separate types of financial institutions.

With this climate of change in the financial services industry and the transparency created by technology and the Internet, many Americans have grown concerned about the accessibility of their personal financial information and how businesses, including banks, might be collecting, maintaining, using, and analyzing this information.

Privacy Regulations

> The right to be let alone—the most comprehensive of rights, and the right most valued by civilized men.
>
> —Justice Louis Brandeis, *Olmstead v. U.S.* (1928)

Personal freedom is an important concern of individuals. The "right to be let alone" could be expanded to include the right of individuals to control how information about them is used.

To implement the GLBA privacy standards, the GLBA required the banking regulatory agencies to issue privacy regulations. These agencies include the:

- Federal Reserve System
- Federal Deposit Insurance Corporation
- Office of the Comptroller of the Currency
- Office of Thrift Supervision

Although the different agencies have issued separate regulations, the requirements are essentially the same.

The GLBA established three main requirements for the privacy protection regulations:

1. *Initial notices.* Banks must develop privacy policies and provide initial notices about them to customers. The policies must describe the conditions under which the bank may disclose nonpublic personal information to nonaffiliated third parties and affiliates. These notices must be accurate, clear, and conspicuous.
2. *Annual notices.* Banks must provide annual notices of their privacy policies to their current customers. These notices must be accurate, clear, and conspicuous.

3. *"Opt-out" provision.* Banks must provide a reasonable method for consumers to opt out of disclosures to nonaffiliated third parties. That is, consumers must be given a reasonable opportunity and means to direct the bank not to disclose the information. Consumers may exercise their opt out right at any time.

The regulations also established other requirements of privacy protection. The regulations specify:

- Required content of the notices and sample clauses
- How the notices can be delivered to individuals and in what form
- Exceptions to the requirements
- Limits on the types of information that can be disclosed

It is widely recognized that consumers are concerned that businesses may release personal information about them without their knowledge and consent. In particular, they are worried about release of their financial records to unknown parties.

Accessible Electronic Records

In the past, personal information that a business collected about a customer was kept on paper records. Retrieving and using the information was laborious, even for the business that collected the information.

Even the idea of dealing with mountains of paper records discouraged sharing much of this information beyond the immediate needs of each business. Record keeping was fragmented, information became quickly outdated, and businesses seldom used the information beyond the original purpose of gathering it.

For example:

A bank would gather substantial information about a loan applicant to make a loan decision, but after that point, much of the personal information was simply stored in the loan file. Because the bank restricted access to the file, the information was kept confidential.

With the development of electronic information storage, banks and other businesses could more easily retrieve filed information, analyze it, and use it for many purposes.

For example: A bank retrieves the names and addresses of deposit account customers and sends these customers a mailing to encourage them to apply for a credit card at the bank.

As long as this information remained within the control of the business that originally collected the information, most customers continued to trust that the business was using the information in a limited and responsible way.

However, electronic data storage has become very sophisticated, and the sharing or release of personal information is becoming much easier and more widespread. Consumers hear horror stories of companies accidentally releasing computer files of information or computer hackers breaking into company systems and stealing information such as credit card numbers.

For the banking industry, the GLBA's provisions are breaking down the barriers among banks, investment companies, and insurance companies and making information sharing even easier.

Consumers see even greater reason to object to widespread sharing of their personal information especially without their knowledge and permission.

Identity Theft

Another area of concern for consumers is identity theft. Criminals steal information about an individual and then assume the person's identity to obtain credit cards, make fraudulent transactions, or otherwise defraud merchants or financial institutions.

To assume the other person's identity, the criminal may obtain the victim's:

- Credit card numbers
- Social security number

- Driver's license number
- Other information

The criminal uses this information to impersonate the victim and obtain cash or credit for purchases. After quickly plundering the victim's credit and destroying his or her reputation, the criminal moves on to another identity.

Although most victims of identity theft are not responsible for paying the bills generated by the criminal, restoring their good name and good credit can be time consuming and exhausting. It can take years to clean up the incorrect charges and financial records. During this time, victims may have difficulty obtaining loans, cashing checks, or performing other transactions.

Identity theft has become a greater threat in recent times because technology has created an environment where thieves often have access to more sources of information about victims. No longer is the theft of a wallet or purse the easiest way for a criminal to obtain credit cards and other information needed to impersonate victims.

Criminals can fraudulently obtain a credit report that contains substantial amounts of personal financial information. Or criminals steal preapproved credit offers from the victim's mail or trash.

Concern about identity theft has made many consumers more protective of their personal information and more selective about who is allowed to use it.

Privacy Policies

Historically, a combination of court decisions, state laws, federal laws, and voluntary policies of banks served to protect the privacy of consumer financial information.

For example, an important federal law governing privacy of financial records is the Right to Financial Privacy Act of 1978. This law establishes the standards for how federal agencies obtain financial records from a bank.

The law provides that certain types of customers must be notified by the government before the bank releases records to the federal agency (with certain exceptions). The exceptions include disclosures in response to judicial subpoenas and administrative subpoenas, and other disclosures required by federal law or regulation.

Although the Right to Financial Privacy Act protects important consumer rights, it has a limited application—it applies only to situations where a federal governmental authority is seeking the information.

Some banks have also adopted voluntary privacy policies. Often these policies are based on voluntary privacy principles developed by banking trade associations.

The bank's first step is to develop its privacy policies (in compliance with other parts of the regulation).

When the bank accomplishes the first step, it is ready to write the initial privacy notice described earlier. After the bank develops the initial privacy notice, regulations require it to provide the notice to the proper recipients. The regulations are specific as to who should receive the notice and when.

Recipients of the initial notice can include both consumers and customers, which the regulations specifically differentiate. A consumer is an individual who obtains or has obtained a financial product or service from a bank that is to be used primarily for personal, family, or household purposes. Therefore, businesses are not included.

TIPS AND TECHNIQUES

Examples of Consumers

Sean . . . applies for a loan to be used for personal, family, or household purposes (even if the loan is not approved).

Gabrielle . . . provides information to a bank in connection with receiving financial, investment, or economic advice (even if a continuing advisory relationship is not established).

Tips and Techniques (continued)

Dina . . . has a mortgage loan in which the bank has ownership or servicing rights (even though another company is hired to handle payment collection).

Examples of Individuals Who Are Not Consumers

Melanie . . . has designated a bank as trustee of a trust.

Laura . . . is a beneficiary of such a trust.

Seth . . . is a participant of an employee benefit plan that is such a trust.

This exclusion might seem surprising, but the commentary on the regulation recognizes that the trust itself is the bank's "customer." Therefore, the rules do not apply because the trust is not an individual.

A "customer relationship" means a continuing relationship between a consumer and a bank under which the bank provides one or more financial products and services to the consumer (primarily for personal, family, or household purposes). Customers can be defined as a subgroup of the bank's consumers (see Exhibit 4.1).

Generally, the initial privacy notice must be provided immediately when the consumer establishes a customer relationship; however, timing of the notice can be delayed in specific circumstances, such as when the notice would substantially delay the customer's transaction.

For example, the person and the bank may have agreed over the phone to begin a customer relationship, and prompt delivery of the service is involved. Another example is the disbursal of a student loan to Tom, without prior communication between Tom and the bank. In these types of cases, the bank must provide the notice within a "reasonable time."

EXHIBIT 4.1

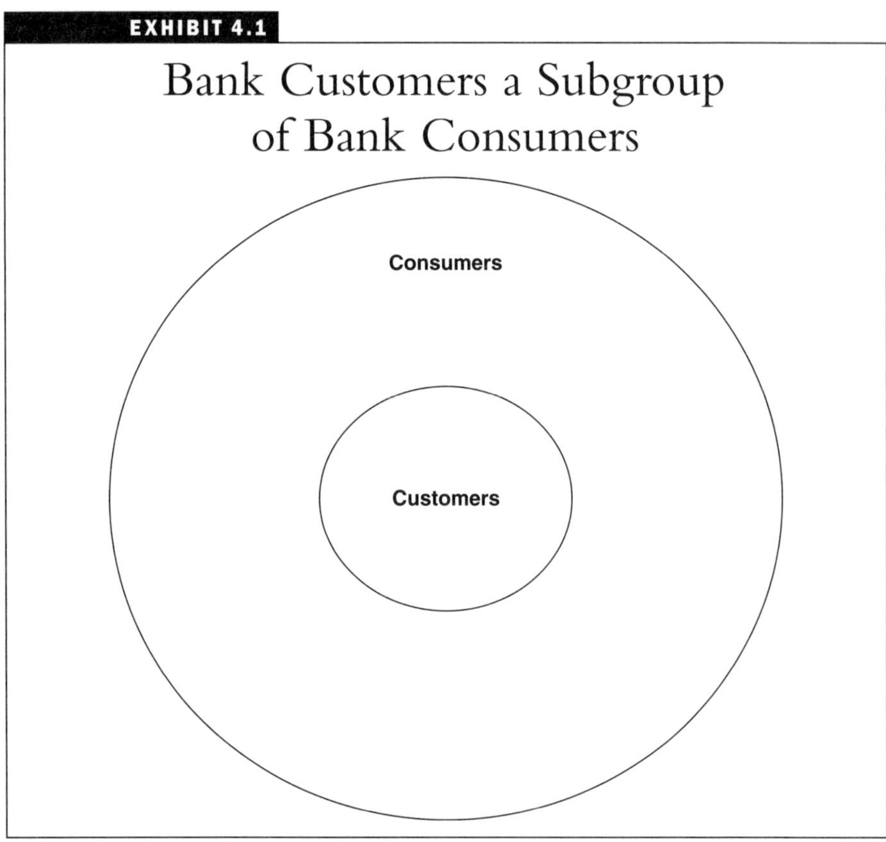

The bank must send a consumer the initial privacy notice before it discloses any nonpublic personal information about the consumer to any nonaffiliated third party (with certain exceptions). Here is where the regulations start getting complex.

The terms "nonpublic personal information" and "nonaffiliated third party" are important in order to understand the requirements of the regulation. Review the chart on page 78 carefully as it defines these important terms.

Examples of personally identifiable financial information include:

- Information Zeke provides to a bank on an application to obtain a loan, credit card, or other financial product or service

- Account balance information, payment history, overdraft history, and credit or debit card purchase information
- The fact that John is or has been one of the bank's customers or has obtained a financial product or service from the bank
- Any information about Wade if it is disclosed in a manner that indicates that he is or has been the bank's customer
- Any information that Tanya provides to a bank or that the bank otherwise obtains in connection with collecting on a loan or servicing a loan
- Any information the bank collects through an Internet "cookie" (an information-collecting device from a web server)
- Information from a consumer report

Sounds like just about anything that a consumer might provide counts as personally identifiable financial information, doesn't it? Well, the regulations specifically note information *not* included as personally identifiable financial information:

- A list of names and addresses of customers of an entity that is not a bank.
- Information that does not identify a consumer, such as aggregate information or blind data that does not contain personal identifiers such as account numbers, names, or addresses.

For example: A bank could extract totals of information from its database, such as the fact that it has processed 2,000 ATM withdrawals last month for consumers who hold accounts at other banks. *This would not be personally identifiable financial information.*

When the regulations refer to "publicly available information," they mean any information that a bank has a reasonable basis to believe is lawfully made available to the general public from:

- Federal, state, or local government records (such as public records of lien filings that show mortgage information)

- Widely distributed media (such as telephone books, newspapers, television, or web sites that are available to the general public)
- Legally required disclosures to the general public

For example: A bank has a reasonable basis to believe that Paul's telephone number is available to the general public if the bank has located the number in the telephone book or if Paul has informed the bank that the number is listed.

Now let's look at what *nonaffiliated third party* means. The regulations define nonaffiliated third party as any person *except*:

- A bank's affiliate
- A person jointly employed by the bank and a company that is not affiliated with the bank

Certain exceptions apply to this requirement on disclosure to nonaffiliated third parties.

To see all the definitions that apply to the requirement on when consumers must receive the initial notice, consider the following:

The bank must send a *consumer* the initial privacy notice . . .	. . . before the bank discloses any *nonpublic personal information* about the consumer . . .	. . . to any *nonaffiliated third party* (with certain exceptions).
Definitions Summary		
Customer:	*Nonpublic personal information:*	*Nonaffiliated third party:*
Individual who obtains or has obtained a financial product or service from a financial institution that is to be used primarily for personal, family, or household purposes.	Personally identifiable financial information, and any list, description, or other grouping of consumers that is derived using any personally identifiable financial information that is not publicly available.	Any person *except* a bank's affiliate, or a person jointly employed by the bank and a company that is not affiliated with the bank.

Definitions Summary

Personally identifiable financial information: Any information a consumer provides to a financial institution to obtain a financial product or service from the institution or that the institution otherwise obtains about that consumer in connection with providing a product.

Publicly available information: Any information that a bank has a reasonable basis to believe is lawfully made available to the general public from federal, state, or local government records, widely distributed media, or legally required disclosures to the general public.

The regulations also require banks to provide an annual privacy notice to customers. The bank must send the notice at least once in any period of 12 consecutive months during the customer relationship.

A bank is not required to provide an annual notice to a former customer without retaining servicing rights.

For the purposes of this book, *standard* notices mean the initial, annual, and revised notices sent by a bank that discloses (or reserves the right to disclose) nonpublic personal information to third parties (outside of the exceptions).

The bank's "standard" privacy notices include seven pieces of information:

1. The categories of nonpublic personal information that the bank collects.
2. The categories of nonpublic personal information that the bank discloses.
3. The categories of third parties to whom the bank discloses the information.
4. The categories of nonpublic personal information about the bank's former customers that it discloses and the categories of third parties to which it discloses this information.
5. An explanation of the consumer's right to opt out of the disclosure of nonpublic personal information to third parties and how to exercise this option.
6. The bank's policies and practices on protecting the confidentiality and security of nonpublic personal information.
7. If a bank discloses nonpublic personal information to third parties under an exception, the bank is required to state only that it makes disclosures to these parties as permitted by law. (The bank is not required to list the exceptions.)

"Simplified" notices are those that the regulations specifically allow if a bank does not disclose (or does not reserve the right to disclose) nonpublic personal information about customers or former customers (outside of the exceptions).

In a simplified notice, the bank must state:

- The fact that the bank does not disclose nonpublic personal information
- The categories of nonpublic personal information that the bank collects

- The bank's policies and practices on respecting the confidentiality and security of nonpublic personal information
- That the bank makes disclosures to other nonaffiliated third parties as allowed by law (if the bank makes disclosures under the exceptions only)

Since the bank does not disclose (or reserve the right to disclose) the restricted information, the opt-out provision does not apply to simplified notices.

The "*short-form*" notice is a special type of initial notice that banks can send to a consumer who is not a customer. The short-form initial notice must:

- Be clear and conspicuous. "Clear and conspicuous" means that a notice is reasonably understandable and designed to call attention to the nature and significance of the information in the notice.
- Be provided at the same time as the bank delivers an opt-out notice as required under the rules for the opt-out notices.
- State that the bank's privacy notice is available upon request.
- Explain a reasonable means by which the consumer may obtain that notice, such as by providing a toll-free telephone number that the consumer may call, or maintaining copies of the notice at the bank's office for consumers who conduct business in person.
- If the consumer requests the bank's privacy notice, the bank must deliver that notice according to the requirements described earlier in this chapter.

The bank also ensures that other elements on the web site (such as text, graphics, hyperlinks, or sound) do not distract attention from the notice.

The bank also calls attention to the nature and significance of the information when it places the notice (or a link to the notice) on a screen that the consumers frequently access, such as a screen on which transactions are conducted. If a link is used, it connects the consumer directly to the notice. The link is labeled appropriately to convey the importance, nature, and relevance of the notice.

Opt-Out Provision

"Opt out" means a direction by the consumer that the bank not disclose nonpublic personal information about that consumer to a nonaffiliated third party (other than the permitted exceptions).

A bank must provide an opportunity for the consumer to opt out. The bank cannot disclose the regulated information if the consumer opts out.

The bank must comply with the opt-out requirement regardless of whether the bank and the consumer have established a customer relationship.

An opt-out notice must be a clear and conspicuous notice to consumers that accurately explains the right to opt out. It must state:

- That the bank discloses or reserves the right to disclose nonpublic personal information about its consumers to a nonaffiliated third party
- That the consumer has the right to opt out of that disclosure
- A reasonable means by which the consumer may exercise the opt-out

The bank must provide a "reasonable means" for the consumer to exercise the opt-out right. A bank may require each consumer to opt out through a specific means, as long as that means is reasonable for that consumer.

However, the regulations establish that the method is unreasonable if the only means of opting out is:

- For the consumer to write his or her own letter to exercise that opt out right

- If any notice subsequent to the initial notice requires the consumer to use a check-off box that the bank provided only with the initial notice

The bank is allowed to provide the opt-out notice with the initial notice or the bank may provide the opt-out notice later than the initial notice. In these cases, the bank must also provide a copy of the initial notice with the opt-out notice in writing or, if the consumer agrees, electronically.

The bank must allow the consumer a "reasonable opportunity" to opt out before the bank discloses the information to the nonaffiliated third party.

For an isolated transaction, such as the purchase of a cashier's check by a consumer, a bank provides the consumer with a reasonable opportunity to opt out if the bank provides the notices at the time the transaction takes place. Here the bank requests that the consumer decide, as a necessary part of the transaction, whether to opt out before completing the transaction.

A bank must comply with a consumer's opt-out direction as soon as reasonably practicable after the bank receives it. In addition, the consumer may exercise the right to opt out at any time after the first opportunity.

A consumer's "direction" to exercise his or her right to "opt out" under the opt-out provisions of the privacy regulations is effective until the consumer revokes it in writing or, if the consumer agrees, electronically.

The opt-out requirements do not apply when a bank provides nonpublic personal information to a nonaffiliated third party to perform services for the bank or functions on the bank's behalf. However, the bank must still supply the initial privacy notice in these situations.

In addition, the bank must enter into a contract with the third party that prohibits the third party from disclosing or using the information other than to carry out the purposes for which the bank provided the information. The type of service the third party performs can include joint marketing of:

- The bank's own products or services
- Financial products and services offered under a joint agreement between the bank and other financial institutions

On occasion, a bank may disclose nonpublic personal information as necessary to "effect, administer, or enforce a transaction" that a consumer requests or authorizes, or in connection with:

- Servicing or processing a financial product or service that a consumer requests or authorizes
- Maintaining or servicing the consumer's account with a bank or with another entity as part of a private label credit card program or other extension of credit on behalf of such entity
- A proposed or actual securitization, secondary market sale (including sales of servicing rights), or similar transaction

In these cases, the requirements for initial notice and opt-out do not apply (if the consumer is not a customer). However, if the consumer is a customer, then the bank is required to send the simplified initial notice.

The regulations explain what it means to "effect, administer, or enforce a transaction," including to:

- Carry out the transaction or maintain the consumer's account in the ordinary course of providing the product or service.
- Enforce the bank's rights (or other party's rights) in carrying out the transaction or providing a service.
- Supply confirmations or other records of the transaction to the consumer.
- Underwrite insurance at the consumer's request or administer the account.

- Administer and audit payment systems such as transactions by debit cards, credit cards, or checks.

(The regulations also provide other specific situations.)

Other exceptions to the requirements for the initial notice or the opt-out provisions apply when a bank discloses nonpublic personal information in these ways:

- With the consent or at the order of the consumer
- To protect the confidentiality or security of a bank's records pertaining to the consumer or service
- To protect against or prevent fraud
- For required institutional risk control or resolving consumer disputes
- To persons holding a legal or beneficial interest relating to the consumer
- To persons acting in a fiduciary or representative capacity on behalf of the consumer
- To provide information to organizations or agencies that are rating the bank or assessing the bank's compliance with industry standards
- To bank examiners, law enforcement agencies, the courts, and similar parties to the extent permitted or required by law (e.g., under the Right to Financial Privacy Act)
- To consumer reporting agencies (or from a consumer report) under the Fair Credit Reporting Act

(Other situations in which an exception applies are given in the regulations.)

For example: Carlos, a consumer who is not a customer, has applied to a bank for a mortgage. He may specifically consent to the bank's disclosure to a nonaffiliated insurance company of the fact that Carlos has applied to the bank for a mortgage so that the insurance company can offer homeowner's insurance to Carlos. In this case, the bank does not send the initial privacy notice nor offer opt-out.

However, if Carlos's loan is approved and he becomes a customer of the bank, then the bank begins sending him the appropriate privacy notices.

The regulations establish exceptions to certain requirements of the regulations. Under these exceptions, the opt-out provision does not apply and notice requirements may not apply.

	Initial Notice Requirement	**Opt-Out Provision**
Service providers and joint marketing	Send initial notice	Does not apply
Processing and servicing transactions	If consumer is *not* a customer: No initial notice If a customer: Send simplified notice	Does not apply
Other exceptions	If consumer is *not* a customer: No initial notice If a customer: Send simplified notice	Does not apply

When considering limits on disclosures, it is important to note whether a particular situation fits into the exceptions or is outside the exceptions.

Situations Where Disclosure Occurs Under the Exceptions

- A bank hires an ad agency to promote a new bank service and the bank discloses a customer list to the agency.
- A bank makes home mortgage loans but hires another company to process payments. The bank must disclose information about the borrowers to the processing company for it to process the payments.
- A bank allows its outside auditing company access to bank records containing nonpersonal public information about consumers so that the auditing company can perform its job.

Disclosure Situations Outside the Exceptions

- A bank sells a customer list to a tax preparation company that wishes to market its services to the bank's customers. The bank only discloses names and addresses of customers who have received privacy notices and who have not opted out of disclosure.
- A bank sells a customer list to a local home improvement company that wishes to market its services to the bank's mortgage customers. The bank only discloses names and addresses of mortgage customers who have received privacy notices and who have not opted out of disclosure.

When considering limits on the redisclosure and reuse of information throughout this section, bear in mind whether:

- The bank is receiving or disclosing information.
- The situation falls under an exception or is outside the exceptions.

In addition to the discussion of the requirements on redisclosure and use of information in this section, Table 4.1 summarizes the requirements.

IN THE REAL WORLD

Second Bank receives a customer list from First Bank, a nonaffiliated bank, in order to provide account-processing services for First Bank.

This disclosure was received under a permitted exception. Second Bank can disclose that information under an exception or as needed to service the accounts.

In this instance, Second Bank could disclose the information to its attorneys, accountants, and auditors, or respond to a subpoena. Second Bank, however, could not disclose the information to a third party for marketing purposes or use that information for its own marketing purposes.

TABLE 4.1

Redisclosure Requirements

If the bank . . .	Receives Information . . .	Discloses Information . . .
Under an exception	The bank may only:	The third party may only:
	Disclose the information to its own affiliates (However, affiliates may disclose and use the information only to the extent that the bank may.)	Disclose the information to its own affiliates (However, affiliates may disclose and use the information only to the extent that the third party may.)
	Disclose the information to the affiliates of the original disclosing institution	Disclose the information to the affiliates of the original disclosing bank
	Disclose and use the information as permitted under an allowed exception to notice and opt-out requirements	Disclose and use the information as permitted under an allowed exception to notice and opt-out requirements
Outside an exception	The bank may only disclose to:	The third party may only disclose to:
	Its own affiliates (However, affiliates may disclose the information only to the extent that the bank may.)	Its own affiliates (However, affiliates may disclose the information only to the extent that the third party may.)
	The affiliates of the original disclosing institution	The affiliates of the disclosing bank
	Any other person, if the disclosure would be lawful if the original disclosing institution made it directly to the person	Any other person, if the disclosure would be lawful if the original disclosing bank made it directly to the person

If a bank receives nonpublic personal information from a nonaffiliated financial institution under an exception, the bank may only:

- Disclose the information to its own affiliates. (However, the affiliates may disclose and use the information only to the extent that the bank may.)
- Disclose the information to the affiliates of the original disclosing institution.
- Disclose and use the information as permitted under an allowed exception to notice and opt out requirements.

If a bank discloses nonpublic personal information to a nonaffiliated third party under an exception, the third party may only:

- Disclose the information to its own affiliates. (However, affiliates may disclose and use the information only to the extent that the third party may.)
- Disclose the information to the affiliates of the original disclosing bank.

IN THE REAL WORLD

Second Bank obtains a customer list from First Bank, a nonaffiliated bank. Second Bank plans to use the list to market its home equity loans to First Bank's customers. (First Bank does not offer home equity loans.)

This disclosure is outside of the allowed exceptions to notice and opt-out requirements. Second Bank may use that list and can disclose that list to Third Bank, another nonaffiliated bank, only if First Bank could have lawfully disclosed the list to Third Bank.

In other words, Second Bank may redisclose the list according to the privacy policy of First Bank (as limited by the opt-out direction of First Bank's consumers). In addition, Second Bank can disclose the list to excepted parties, such as its attorneys or accountants.

- Disclose and use the information as permitted under an allowed exception to notice and opt-out requirements.

If a bank receives nonpublic personal information from a nonaffiliated financial institution outside of an exception, the bank may disclose the information only to:

- Its own affiliates (However, affiliates may disclose the information only to the extent that the bank may.)
- The affiliates of the original disclosing institution
- Any other person, if the disclosure would be lawful if the original disclosing institution made it directly to the person

If a bank discloses nonpublic personal information to a nonaffiliated third party outside of an exception, the third party may disclose the information only to:

- Its own affiliates (However, affiliates may disclose the information only to the extent that the third party may.)
- The affiliates of the disclosing bank
- Any other person, if the disclosure would be lawful if the original disclosing bank made it directly to the person

The regulations are particularly restrictive on sharing account numbers for marketing purposes. A bank (or its affiliates) must not disclose an account number or similar form of access number or access code for a consumer's account (credit card, deposit account, or transaction account) to any nonaffiliated third party (outside the exceptions described later) for:

- Telemarketing
- Direct mail marketing
- Marketing through electronic mail to the consumer

According to the regulations, "account number" does *not* include a number or code in an encrypted form, as long as the bank does not provide the recipient with a means to decode the number or code.

The regulations make these exceptions to this restriction on account number sharing for marketing purposes:

- Consumer reporting agencies
- The bank's agents or service providers solely for marketing the bank's own products or services, as long as they are not authorized to initiate charges to the account
- Participants in a private label credit card program or an affinity or similar program where the participants are identified to the customer

Right to Financial Privacy

Privacy

With the passage of the Privacy Act, Congress originally addressed the idea of a need to protect citizens' rights with regard to government access to financial records in 1974. It strengthened citizens' rights with passage of the Right to Financial Privacy Act of 1978.

The Right to Financial Privacy Act

The Right to Financial Privacy Act governs government authority access to financial records and other financial information maintained by financial institutions. The intent of the Act is to address concerns that government agencies were gaining access to citizens' private financial information without due process.

- The Right to Financial Privacy Act does not enlarge or restrict any rights of a financial institution to challenge requests for records made by a government authority.
- The Right to Financial Privacy Act does not entitle a customer to assert the rights of a financial institution.

On receipt of a request for financial records made by a government authority, pursuant to the Right to Financial Privacy Act, a financial institution must:

- Proceed to assemble the records requested.
- Prepare to deliver the records to the government authority.

Use of Information

Financial records originally obtained using the Right to Financial Privacy Act *must not be transferred to another agency or department* unless the transferring agency or department certifies in writing that there is reason to believe the records are relevant to a legitimate law enforcement inquiry within the jurisdiction of the receiving agency or department.

- The Right to Financial Privacy Act does not prohibit the disclosure of financial records or other financial information that is not directly identifiable with or identifiable as being delivered from the financial records of a particular customer.
- The Right to Financial Privacy Act does not apply to a legitimate law enforcement inquiry.
- The Right to Financial Privacy Act does not apply to a subpoena or court order arising out of any grand jury proceedings.

In the case where the court may find that there is reason to believe that notifying the customer might result in endangering the lives or physical safety of a customer or group of customers, the court may order an indefinite delay in customer notification.

Should a government authority use these special procedures, that authority must provide the financial institution a certification signed by a supervisory official of the rank designated by the authority certifying that the request is in compliance with the Right to Financial Privacy Act.

Within five days following access to the financial records, the government authority must file, with the appropriate court, a signed and sworn statement issued by a supervisory official of the rank designated by the authority. This statement must disclose the basis for the emergency access.

Any further actions by the requesting government authority will necessitate compliance with the customer notice provisions of the Right to Financial Privacy Act.

Cost Reimbursement

The Board of Governors of the Federal Reserve System establishes the rate of reimbursement to financial institutions, their costs of producing the financial records, and other financial information provided under the Right to Financial Privacy Act.

Penalties

Financial institutions and/or government authorities that obtain or disclose financial records or financial information in violation of the Right to Financial Privacy Act are liable to the customer to whom the records relate for an amount equal to:

- $100 without regard to the volume of records released
- Actual damages sustained by the customer as a result of the disclosure
- Any punitive damages the court may allow if the violation was willful and intentional
- The costs of any action brought to enforce liability under the Right to Financial Privacy Act
- Reasonable attorney's fees, as established by the court

Summary

Bank regulators are responsible for monitoring compliance with consumer protection laws. The consumer protection regulations most likely to be encountered in banking are the Expedited Funds Availability Act, Truth in Savings, Electronic Fund Transfer, Equal Credit Opportunity, Truth in Lending, and Privacy of Financial Information.

The Expedited Funds Availability Act is a law enacted by Congress and implemented through Regulation CC of the Federal Reserve Board. It was enacted to speed up the collection of checks and other items deposited to transaction accounts.

Regulation DD implements Truth in Savings, which was enacted to help consumers make informed decisions about deposit accounts at banking institutions. This regulation allows consumers to make comparisons among banks by requiring that consumers receive disclosures of information such as balance requirements, interest rates, and penalties (if any) and fees.

The Electronic Fund Transfer Act, implemented under Regulation E, establishes the basic rights, liabilities, and responsibilities of consumers who transfer funds electronically and the financial institutions that offer these services.

Another regulation, the Equal Credit Opportunity Act, implemented under Regulation B, is designed to assure that all creditworthy applicants are treated fairly regardless of race, color, religion, national origin, sex, marital status, age, or income from public assistance.

Truth in Lending promotes the informed use of consumer credit by requiring disclosures about terms and costs of credit. Regulation Z implements Truth in Lending and requires written disclosures on the cost of the loan or other credit, places restrictions on the terms of home mortgages, and regulates certain credit card practices.

Congress passed the Privacy Act in 1974 to address the need to protect citizens from government access to financial records and strengthened citizens' rights with the passage of the Right to Financial Privacy

Act of 1978. Neither act regulates the release of information to other third parties.

With the passage of the Gramm-Leach-Bliley Act in 1999, further privacy regulations were enacted. Under GLBA, banking regulatory agencies, such as the Federal Reserve System, the Federal Deposit Insurance Corporation, the Office of the Comptroller of the Currency, and the Office of Thrift Supervision, issue privacy regulations requiring that banks disclose their privacy policies to consumers initially and annually in an accurate, clear, and conspicuous fashion. In addition, banks must provide consumers with an opportunity to opt out regarding the disclosure of information to nonaffiliated third parties.

The privacy protection regulations are complex for a bank that discloses restricted information to third parties. However, the banking industry must consider the consumer's frame of reference. Consumers are justifiably worried about the privacy of their personal information, and the banking industry has the responsibility to satisfy these concerns.

CHAPTER 5

The Business of Banking and the Bank Secrecy Act

After reading this chapter, you will be able to:

- Understand the role of the Bank Secrecy Act in preventing criminal activity.
- Explain who must comply with the Act and why.
- Discuss the BSA and a safe banking system.
- Describe money laundering and how to prevent it.

In this chapter we'll learn about the Bank Secrecy Act—how it affects the business of banking from A to Z.

In 1970, after extensive congressional hearings about the unavailability of bank records of individuals suspected of criminal activities,

Congress took action. The Bank Secrecy Act (BSA) was enacted that year.

The Supreme Court upheld the BSA as constitutional in 1974, in the case of *California Bankers Association v. Shultz*. When the constitutionality of the Act was challenged in court, the Supreme Court noted that it was examining the constitutionality of the regulations, since the BSA itself imposed no penalties on anyone. Only those who violate specific regulations are subject to civil and criminal penalties.

The BSA establishes a framework for record keeping and reporting that is required particularly by banks, but also by many nonbanking financial institutions (NBFIs) such as securities brokers, dealers registered with the Securities and Exchange Commission, casinos, currency exchangers, money transmitters (such as Western Union), and, in some cases, even private individuals.

Since the BSA was first passed, Congress and the regulatory agencies have made numerous modifications to help ease the sometimes onerous regulatory burden and to increase its effectiveness. The BSA was passed by Congress, but the U.S. Department of the Treasury implements the regulations that give the Act "teeth."

The Office of the Comptroller of the Currency (OCC) is the regulatory agency that oversees national banks' adherence to the BSA.

Other regulatory agencies that may be involved include:

- Internal Revenue Service (IRS)
- FinCEN (Financial Crimes Enforcement Network)
- Customs
- Immigration and Naturalization Service (INS)
- Securities and Exchange Commission (SEC)
- Federal Reserve Board (the Fed)
- Federal Deposit Insurance Corporation (FDIC)
- Office of Thrift Supervision (OTS)
- National Credit Union Administration (NCUA)

Additionally, various parties are involved in creating, amending, implementing, and enforcing the BSA. In enacting the BSA, Congress has recognized the "gatekeeper" role banks have in helping to prevent facilitating criminal transactions. Essentially, the main purpose of the BSA is to trace illicit transactions. Prior to the BSA, there were very few rules and regulations in place to help prevent or detect money laundering.

Money Laundering and the Law in Brief

The United States was one of the first countries to introduce tough legislation specifically designed to prevent money laundering. Many other countries have followed suit, and now nearly 100 countries have legislation and regulations to help prevent money laundering.

The goal of the BSA is to identify the source, volume, and movement of currency and other monetary instruments, either into or out of the United States or being deposited in financial institutions. Law enforcement and regulatory agencies are then able to use the information that is reported under the Act to investigate criminal, tax, and regulatory violations.

Simply stated, money laundering is concealing and/or moving illegally generated cash with the purpose of creating the appearance of legitimate funds.

Money launderers use various schemes with many degrees of complexity. In general, money laundering consists of three stages:

1. Placement
2. Layering
3. Integration

"Placement" can be defined as the movement of funds from illegal activities into legitimate financial institutions or the retail economy.

For example, a drug dealer depositing funds from a drug deal into a bank account is an example of the initial placement stage. Because large deposits attract more attention (and deposits over $10,000 require the bank to fill out a Currency Transaction Report), any actions at this stage may involve relatively small transactions.

In the next stage, *layering*, a money launderer attempts to scramble the origin of the funds, such as by conducting numerous wire transfers to different accounts, to make it difficult to trace the origin of the funds. Illicit funds may be mingled with money obtained through legitimate business transactions.

In the final stage, *integration*, a money launderer brings the money back into the economy, such as by purchasing homes, businesses, vehicles, and jewelry.

At all times, the money launderer (or perhaps a consortium of money launderers, depending on the setup) must maintain control of the proceeds.

Since the volume of cash or other funds is likely to be very high, money launderers tend to divide up the monies into small enough amounts so as not to arouse suspicion.

Banking After the Bank Secrecy Act

Since the BSA's inception in 1970, Congress has continued to strengthen laws against money laundering and to focus on actions that combat money laundering. For example, the Money Laundering Control Act (MLCA) passed in 1986 allows for severe penalties for persons who:

- Knowingly spend money or attempt to spend money obtained from a criminal offense (such as drug dealing).
- Attempt to avoid the reporting requirements.
- Engage in tax evasion in respect to such monies.
- Promote the unlawful activity.

The USA PATRIOT Act of 2001, enacted after the terrorist attacks of that year, further strengthened money-laundering laws by:

- Requiring that all banks and many other financial institutions establish and implement anti-money-laundering training programs for employees
- Extending the "Know Your Customer" requirements
- Extending suspicious activity reporting
- Setting out specific requirements with respect to foreign correspondent banks of U.S. financial institutions

Financial crimes like money laundering inevitably result in a large loss of tax revenues. Money that should rightfully belong in the U.S. economy is spirited offshore. The BSA helps make all applicable transactions taxable as they should be in addition to helping make illicit activities less profitable. The BSA is not perfect, however; it results in an increased regulatory burden, and many legitimate transactions are reported.

Also, what about customers who have nefarious purposes in mind? Won't they just find more "creative" ways around the BSA? Yes, money launderers frequently develop new methods to escape government scrutiny.

Introduction to Record Keeping and Reporting Under the BSA

In order to achieve their goal of reducing money laundering, regulatory agencies require an extensive paper trail of transactions. Record keeping and reporting are an integral part of complying with regulations, and the Bank Secrecy Act is no exception.

Currency Transaction Reports (CTRs) and Suspicious Activity Reports (SARs) are the most common forms that banks have to fill out. The Internal Revenue Service maintains a database of these forms, and the results of computerized analysis are made available to law enforcement.

A CTR has to be filed for transactions involving more than $10,000 in currency. Under the BSA, each financial institution must file a CTR for each of these transactions that involve an amount greater than $10,000 in currency:

- Deposit
- Withdrawal
- Exchange of currency
- Other payment or transfer

Filing CTRs is a serious business; FinCEN is in earnest about enforcing these requirements.

Suspicious Activity Reports

Suspicious Activity Reports (SARs) are to be used for:

- Specifically defined activities
- Banking transactions that may not fall into any specific category but that nevertheless appear suspicious

SARs also help alert officials to patterns of behavior and to specific transactions. All banks are required by regulation to report suspected crimes and suspicious transactions that involve potential money laundering or violate the BSA.

FinCEN published a list of situations that should result in a SAR being filed:

- Continued payments or withdrawals of currency in amounts just under the reporting threshold
- Refusal to provide information needed to keep required records and generate required reports
- Transactions canceled when the customer is informed of reporting requirements
- Funds transfers, payments, or withdrawals that are not consistent with the customer's stated activity of business

- Transfers or receipt of funds without normal identification information about both the source and/or the recipient
- Repeated use of an account as a temporary resting place

Before the SAR system was introduced, the system for reporting suspicious activity was much more unwieldy.

The main problems banks perceive with filing CTRs and SARs are that:

- The sheer volume of forms required is burdensome.
- Even innocent transactions are reported.
- The requirement to report "suspicious" activity is vague and subject to uncertainty.

Many bank customers insist on knowing whether information about them is being reported. Banks cannot answer questions of this type, whether the person in question has been reported or not.

Record-Keeping Issues

Money launderers will provide incomplete, inaccurate, and misleading information to banks. Bankers hope that extensive record-keeping requirements will allow patterns to emerge that show when money launderers are using the banking system. The balancing act that governmental regulatory agencies must consider, however, is that excessive record-keeping requirements are administratively and financially onerous for banks and other institutions and that these costs will be passed on to the consumer.

All financial institutions that are subject to the BSA regulations are also subject to the record-keeping rules for funds transfers and transmittals of funds. The requirement 31 CFR Part 103 applies to:

- Wire transfers
- Internal transfers, if the originator transfers funds from the originator's account to the beneficiary's account at the same bank

- Orders for fund transfers made by other means, including telephone, fax, and e-mail, that are sent or delivered by a customer or on behalf of a customer by a nonbanking financial institution

CFR defines "originator" as the person (whether an individual or corporation) that originates the funds transfer. "Beneficiary" is the person (again whether individual or corporate) that receives the funds that have been transferred. The "originator's bank" is the bank from which the originator initiates the funds transfer. And the "beneficiary's bank" is the bank that receives the funds for the beneficiary.

If the funds transfer is taking place between a domestic institution and a foreign institution, the domestic institution does not need to contact the foreign institution for information that would otherwise be necessary to complete the required forms.

However, the PATRIOT Act does require that banks conduct due diligence prior to establishing correspondent accounts of foreign banks. For example, if the foreign bank is not publicly traded, the U.S. bank must take reasonable steps to identify the owners of the foreign bank. If the foreign bank has correspondent relationships with other foreign banks, the U.S. bank must also make reasonable efforts to determine the ownership of those banks.

The PATRIOT Act goes further to prohibit establishment or maintenance of correspondent accounts with shell banks (those banks that fall under no jurisdiction because they have no physical presence).

One possible way for money launderers to get around record-keeping requirements has been to use accounts with multiple names on them. The regulations require, however, that a bank be able to access records by all of the names on the account, not just the primary account holder.

Another issue for banks is who is to be indicated as the originator if an individual is transferring funds at the behest of a corporate entity. One or more individuals may be authorized to order funds transfers through the corporation's account. In that case, the corporation is the originator, not the individual who orders the transfer.

The Right to Financial Privacy Act (RFPA) makes it illegal, with several exceptions, for the federal government to access a customer's bank records without notification to the customer, unless a customer authorizes the access in writing or the records are disclosed in response to a subpoena, search warrant, or written request. The PATRIOT Act, however, protects a bank from civil liability for voluntarily disclosing suspicious activity to the federal government.

The RFPA covers much of the same subject area as the BSA, but the two statutes are not in conflict. The BSA requires the bank to observe and report both specifically described activities and activities that seem suspicious, and the RFPA limits the federal government's access to customer records.

Who's Exempt from the BSA

Given the number of transactions that involve over $10,000, it would result in an unmanageable flow of documentation if all of these transactions had to be reported and then analyzed by governmental agencies.

Corporations do payroll, sign leases, purchase properties, and perform other actions that regularly require large outlays of cash. Thus, the Secretary of the Treasury identified certain exemptions from the bank's typical requirement to file a CTR for currency transactions involving more than $10,000.

Initially, an *exempt person* was defined as:

- A bank (wherever chartered) to the extent of its United States activities
- A federal, state, or local government department or agency
- Any entity exercising governmental authority (such as the power to tax, to exercise eminent domain, or to exercise police powers)
- Any corporation whose common stock is listed on the New York Stock Exchange or the American Stock Exchange (but not the

Emerging Company Market) or the Nasdaq National Market (but not the Nasdaq Small-Cap Issues Market)

- Any subsidiary of any listed exempt corporation if it filed a consolidated federal income tax

These exemption criteria left out a number of legitimate businesses that regularly engage in transactions involving more than $10,000. Thus, in 1998, additional rules for "exempt" customers were introduced. Under this rule, banks may exempt large currency transactions with a "non-listed business" or "payroll customer" that:

- Has maintained a transaction account with the bank for at least 12 months
- Has frequent currency transactions more than $10,000, or withdraws in excess of $10,000 in currency to pay employees in the United States
- Is incorporated or registered, as an eligible business, in the United States

Consumers are very concerned about financial privacy, and wish to preserve as much of it as possible. By increasing the number of exemptions, banks will have to report fewer transactions, thus helping to preserve privacy.

Once a bank has determined that a customer is exempt, it cannot be penalized for failure to file a CTR, with a couple of exceptions. If the bank, however, knowingly files a false or incomplete report, or if the bank knew or had reason to know that the exempt customer did not conduct the transaction in question, the bank can be penalized.

Just as a bank would take steps to ensure that a customer is not defrauding them, a bank must take similar steps to ensure that a customer is actually exempt.

Note that a customer need not have an account at the bank in order to be classified as exempt. As noted by FinCEN, for example, governmental agencies frequently cash large checks at banks at which they do not have accounts.

Simply because a customer is exempt from a bank requirement to file a CTR does *not* mean that the customer's activities are not suspicious. Thus, the customer's activities may still require that a SAR be filed.

Defining "Funds Transfer"

Do payment orders and letters of credit constitute a funds transfer? In general, an instruction to a bank to pay out under a letter of credit is subject to a requirement that a beneficiary perform specific actions, such as deliver documents. The term "payment order" is limited to instructions that do not require the beneficiary to perform a specific action or fulfill a certain condition. Thus, under these circumstances, an instruction to pay out under a letter of credit is not a funds transfer and is not subject to the rules for fund transfers. However, certain transactions may fall within the definition of payment order.

Note, though, that it may be possible for a money launderer to take advantage of this provision in order to effect sham payment orders and letters of credit with an unscrupulous (possibly offshore) bank. If the domestic bank involved in the transaction suspects this is the case, it would have to file a SAR.

Structuring is an attempt to evade the reporting requirements by breaking up a transaction that would otherwise exceed $10,000 (and thus require a CTR to be filed). Structured transactions can be ambiguous. There is no requirement for a bank to specifically prevent a customer from engaging in this type of activity. The only requirement is that the bank reports this activity.

Although some transactions may be ambiguous as to possible structuring issues, some seem pretty clear-cut. Here are a few examples provided by FinCEN:

- In one case, a customer who identified herself as a housewife made a total of 94 currency deposits, most of which were in amounts slightly under the CTR reporting threshold of $10,000. In total, these amounted to $637,000 over a two-year period.

- A customer made a deposit, in $100 bills, which was just under the reporting threshold. The teller noted the customer was filling out another deposit slip for another account at the same bank. When told of the CTR requirement later that day, the customer canceled a transaction involving a deposit for the same amount, also in $100 bills, at a second branch of the same bank.
- Three individuals made deposits to a single account in less than one hour, all at different branches of the bank. These deposits together totaled more than $10,000. None of the depositors was the account holder.

Bank Examiners' Role in the BSA

Bank examiners are looking for suspicious behavior and circumstances within the bank itself, while a bank should be looking for suspicious behavior and circumstances regarding its customers. In general, if something looks out of place, examiners will want to know why. Presuming that your bank is not participating in money laundering, you should have well-documented answers to any questions a bank examiner is likely to ask and well-organized records for any issue the examiner wants to look at closely.

What are some things an examiner will look for to help determine if a bank is engaged in money laundering? Here is a listing from the bank examiner's manual:

- Increase in cash shipments that are not accompanied by a corresponding increase in the number of accounts.
- Cash on hand frequently exceeds limits established in security program and/or blanket bond coverage.
- Large volume of wire transfers to and from offshore banks.
- Large volume of cashier's checks, money orders, or traveler's checks sold for cash.

- Accounts that have a large number of small deposits and a small number of large checks with the balance of the account remaining relatively low and constant. (Account has many of the same characteristics as an account used for check kiting.)
- A large volume of deposits to several different accounts with frequent transfers of major portion of the balance to a single account at the same bank or at another bank.
- Loans to offshore companies.
- A large volume of cashier's checks or money orders deposited to an account where the nature of the account holder's business would not appear to justify such activity.
- Large volume of cash deposits from a business that is not normally cash intensive.
- Cash deposits to a correspondent bank account by any means other than through an armored carrier.
- Large turnover in large bills or excess of small bills from the bank and demand for large bills by that bank which would appear uncharacteristic for the bank.
- Cash shipments which appear large in comparison to the dollar volume of Currency Transaction Reports (CTRs) filed.
- Dollar limits on the list of the bank customers exempt from currency transaction reporting requirements which appear unreasonably high considering the type and location of the business. No information is in the bank's files to support the limits set.
- CTRs, when filed, are often incorrect or lack important information.
- List of exempted customers appears unusually long.
- High volume of sequentially numbered traveler's checks or postal money orders addressed to same payee.

Of course, a bank probably still is used by money launderers, even if none of these factors applies.

However, all of these issues can be remedied with a good compliance program in place. If proper documentation is provided as to the reasons any of these issues are occurring, the bank examiner is likely not to see them as a problem. For example, if a bank primarily services large corporations, its list of exempted customers may appear long, but it will have a good explanation for the length of the list.

Creating a Compliance Program

Another important thing banks must do to assist them in complying with the BSA is to develop a compliance program. In 1987, the OCC introduced four requirements for compliance programs:

1. Provide for a system of internal controls to assure ongoing compliance.
2. Provide for independent testing for compliance to be conducted by bank personnel or by an outside party.
3. Designate an individual or individuals responsible for coordinating and monitoring day-to-day compliance.
4. Provide training for appropriate personnel.

In general, a bank examiner will look carefully at offshore transactions to determine if there are any unresolved inconsistencies or if there are any suspicious activities.

The information that follows was taken from the Federal Reserve Board's examination manual. This is information you should consider in respect to offshore transactions.

- Loans made on the strength of a borrower's financial statement reflect major investments in and income from businesses incorporated in bank secrecy haven countries.
- Loans to offshore companies.
- Loans secured by obligations of offshore banks.
- Transactions involving an offshore "shell" bank whose name may be very similar to the name of a major legitimate institution.
- Frequent wire transfers of funds to and from bank secrecy haven countries.

- Offers of multimillion-dollar deposits at below-market rates from a confidential source to be sent from an offshore bank or somehow guaranteed by an offshore bank through a letter, telex, or other "official" communication.
- Presence of telex or facsimile equipment in a bank where the usual and customary business activity would not appear to justify the need for such equipment.

Obviously, if a bank provides adequate justification for any of these transactions, that will help considerably in the examination process. However, many of the points listed will remain suspicious no matter the explanation offered. Also, note that the PATRIOT Act now prohibits banks and other financial institutions from establishing or maintaining correspondent accounts with shell banks that have no physical location.

The information that follows was taken from the Federal Reserve Board's examination manual.

What are some suspicious things that a bank examiner looks for in respect to wire transfers?

Again, the overriding rule is that if something does not seem to make sense for the bank's business practices, the examiner will likely scrutinize it carefully. The bank should document anything that might otherwise appear suspicious, and all paperwork should be in order.

- Indications of frequent overrides of established approval authority and other internal controls.
- Intentional circumvention of approval authority by splitting transactions.
- Wire transfers to and from bank secrecy haven countries.
- Frequent or large wire transfers for persons who have no account relationship with bank.
- In a linked financing situation, a borrower's request for immediate wire transfer of loan proceeds to one or more of the banks where the funds for the brokered deposits originated.
- Large or frequent wire transfers against uncollected funds.
- Wire transfers involving cash where the amount exceeds $10,000.

- Inadequate control of password access.
- Customer complaints and/or frequent error conditions.

The list of what a bank examiner looks for in respect to lending, financing, and brokered transactions similarly involves practices that seem suspicious, and which indicate a close connection to banks in jurisdictions known to practice money laundering.

The following information was taken from the Federal Reserve Board's examination manual.

> The following is information you should consider as indications of suspicious lending practices:
>
> - Out-of-territory lending.
> - Loan production used as a basis for officer bonuses.
> - Evidence of unsolicited attempts to buy or re-capitalize the bank where there is evidence of a request for large loans at or about the same time by persons previously unknown to the bank. Promise of large dollar deposits may also be involved.
> - Promise of large dollar deposits in consideration for favorable treatment on loan requests. (Deposits are not pledged as collateral for the loans.)
> - Brokered deposit transactions where the broker's fees are paid for from the proceeds of related loans.
> - Anytime a bank seriously considers a loan request where the bank would have to obtain brokered deposits to be able to fund the loan should be viewed with suspicion.
> - Solicitation by persons who purportedly have access to multi-millions of dollars, from a confidential source, readily available for loans and/or deposits in U.S. financial institutions.
> - Rates and terms quoted are usually more favorable than funds available through normal sources. A substantial fee may be requested in advance or the solicitor may suggest that the fee be paid at closing but demand compensation for expenses, often exceeding $50,000.
> - Prepayment of interest on deposit accounts where such deposit accounts are used as collateral for loans.

"Know Your Customer" Policy

Each of the federal banking agencies encourages banks to create a "Know Your Customer" policy. The banking agencies provide only guidelines to help banks create their own unique policy. Each institution should adopt procedures best suited for its own operation.

The Fed's objectives of a "Know Your Customer" policy are stated next.

A "Know Your Customer" policy should:

- Increase the likelihood that the financial institution is in compliance with all statutes and regulations and adheres to sound and recognized banking practices
- Decrease the likelihood that the financial institution will become a victim of illegal activities perpetrated by its "customers"
- Protect the good name and reputation of the financial institution
- NOT interfere with the relationship of the financial institution with its good customers

Most potential customers appear legitimate, but in reality there are folks out there that want to conduct illicit activities.

The Federal Reserve provides four principles when creating a "Know Your Customer" policy:

1. Make a reasonable effort to determine the true identity of all customers requesting the bank's services.
2. Take particular care to identify the ownership of all accounts and of those using safe-custody facilities.
3. Obtain identification from all new customers and from customers seeking to conduct significant business transactions.
4. Be aware of any unusual transaction activity or activity that is disproportionate to the customer's known business.

A key consideration is to satisfactorily establish the identity of a potential customer *before* starting a business relationship with them.

The next overview of the general principles to follow when establishing customer relationships is also from the Fed.

Personal Accounts:

1. No account should be opened without satisfactory identification such as:
   a. A driver's license with a photograph issued by the state in which the bank is located; OR
   b. A U.S. passport or alien registration card together with:
      i. A college photo identification card
      ii. A major credit card (verify the current status)
      iii. An employer identification card
      iv. An out-of-state driver's license
2. Consider the customer's residence or place of business. If it is not in the area served by the bank or branch, ask why the customer is opening an account at that location.
3. Follow up with calls to the customer's residence or place of employment thanking the customer for opening the account. Disconnected phone service or no record of employment warrant further investigation.
4. Consider the source of funds used to open the account. Large cash deposits should be questioned.
5. For large accounts, ask the customer for a prior bank reference and write a letter to the bank asking about the customer.
6. Check with the service bureaus for indications that the customer has been involved in questionable activities such as kiting incidents and NSF (non-sufficient funds) situations.
7. The identity of the customer may be established through an existing relationship with the institution such as some type of loan or other account relationship.
8. A customer may be a referral from a bank employee or one of the bank's accepted customers. In this instance, a referral alone is not sufficient to identify the customer, but in most instances it should warrant less vigilance than otherwise required.

Business Accounts:

1. Business principals should provide evidence of legal status (e.g. sole proprietorship, partnership, or incorporation or association) when opening a business account.
2. Check the name of a commercial enterprise with a reporting agency and check prior bank references.
3. Follow up with calls to the customer's business thanking the customer for opening the account. Disconnected phone service warrants further investigation.
4. When circumstances allow, perform a visual check of the business to verify the actual existence of the business and that the business has the capability of providing the services described.
5. Consider the source of funds used to open the account. Large cash deposits should be questioned.
6. For large commercial accounts, the following information should be obtained:
   a. A financial statement of the business;
   b. A description of the customer's principal line of business;
   c. A list of major suppliers and customers and their geographic locations;
   d. A description of the business's primary trade area, and whether international transactions are expected to be routine; and
   e. A description of the business operations, i.e., retail versus wholesale, and the anticipated volume of cash sales.
7. Obtain sufficient identification:
   a. Ask for two pieces of ID when an account is opened (one primary and one secondary).
   b. Ask for home and work numbers.
   c. Ask for the customer's previous address.
   d. Require sole proprietors to swear an affidavit regarding their identity and business.

As of April 30, 2003, the Department of the Treasury—in accordance with the PATRIOT Act—requires that all banks institute a

Customer Identification Program (CIP). Some flexibility is allowed the banks as to which documents are used to verify identification, but all banks must have a CIP program that implements reasonable procedures to:

- Collect identifying information about customers opening an account.
- Verify that the customers are who they say they are.
- Maintain records of the information used to verify their identity.
- Determine whether the customer appears on any list of suspected terrorists or terrorist organizations.

Summary

The Bank Secrecy Act (BSA) was first enacted in 1970. Congress and the regulatory agencies have made numerous modifications since then, including the USA PATRIOT Act, which was signed into law October 26, 2001, and provisions, reauthorized in 2005 and 2006. The BSA established rules and regulations to prevent criminals from utilizing the services of banks to facilitate money laundering and other criminal transactions.

To prevent money laundering and the financing of terrorism, the BSA has extensive record-keeping and reporting requirements. Banks must report transactions involving more than $10,000 in currency and suspicious transactions of any size. A Currency Transaction Report (CTR) is filed when a deposit, withdrawal, exchange of currency, or other payment or transfer exceeds $10,000. Certain customers with a long-standing, legitimate need to withdraw or deposit large sums of money (such as for payroll) are exempt from this requirement. Banks are required to file a Suspicious Activity Report (SAR) for specifically defined activities and for transactions that appear otherwise to be suspicious.

What is money laundering? Money laundering is any attempt to conceal or illegally move cash with the purpose of creating the appearance of legitimate funds. Money laundering generally consists of three stages: placement, layering, and integration.

Placement is the movement of funds from illegal activities into legitimate financial institutions or the retail economy. An example is a drug dealer who deposits the proceeds of drug sales into a bank account. In this case, attempts are often made to keep the transactions small to avoid triggering a CTR. However, if the bank follows the "Know Your Customer" provisions of the Act, suspicious transactions that are below the threshold are likely to trigger a SAR. The second stage of money laundering is layering, where the money launderer attempts to disguise the origin of funds by conducting various wire transfers to different accounts or mingling legitimate business transactions with fraudulent transactions. Integration is the stage where the money launderer attempts to bring the funds back into the economy by purchasing homes, businesses, vehicles, jewelry, and the like.

Another way money launderers attempt to evade reporting requirements is by structuring, a sometimes complex activity that generally involves breaking up a transaction that would otherwise exceed the $10,000 threshold. A bank is not required to prevent structuring; however, it must report it.

One way to prevent money laundering is to have a "Know Your Customer" policy. A good policy involves making a reasonable effort to determine the true identity of all customers, taking care to identify the ownership of all accounts, and obtaining proper identification from all new customers and those seeking to conduct significant business transactions. The most important consideration is to satisfactorily establish the identity of a potential customer *before* starting a business relationship.

CHAPTER 6

The Banker: Knowledge, Skills, and Attitude

After reading this chapter, you will be able to:

- Understand the role of business development in the marketing process.
- List and detail the steps in the business development cycle.
- Demonstrate knowledge of how to successfully close a sale.

In the last several chapters, we have covered the basic business of banking and the regulatory environment in which it operates. This chapter will familiarize you with the sales and marketing process and introduce critical skills needed to be a successful business developer.

Business development is a key component of the marketing process. It includes all aspects of the sales process—from prospect development to closing the sale and establishing the customer relationship.

The job of business development can be stated simply. It is to make the sale—to get in front of prospects, discover the goods and services they need, and make the presentation that results in a business relationship.

Marketing versus Business Development

Marketing can be defined as the entire strategic process of planning and executing the conception, and pricing, promotion, and distribution of ideas, goods, and services. Marketing is the "big picture." It establishes what your business is selling and determines pricing, promotion, and distribution.

Business development is the "frontline" effort. It carries the marketing message to prospects, presents the product as a solution to needs, and wins the business and establishes the client relationship.

Preparation and Readiness for Sales

Many people shy away from business development because they fear rejection. Yet there are many techniques that can improve a person's sales effectiveness and reduce his or her fear of rejection. The first technique is being physically and mentally prepared for sales.

Physical and Mental Preparation for Sales

Selling is the process of helping customers to make satisfying buying decisions. Selling requires you to prepare physically and mentally to hear what the customer wants and needs and then successfully match customer desires with the features of the products offered for sale.

Appearance helps form the prospect's first impression of you and your company. Dress should communicate:

- Readiness to conduct business
- Professionalism
- Comfort in the customer's environment

What Else Does It Take to Be Successful?

Here are the key elements:

- Know and believe in your product.
- Have empathy with the customer.
- Set goals.
- Create and follow a solid work plan.
- Be prepared.

Know and Believe in Your Product. The first step of the sales process is to know the product you're selling. Learn everything there is to know about your product or service. You must be able to answer these questions:

- *What is it?* (features and differences with competing products)
- *What is the idea behind it?* (reason for development, its developer)
- *How does it help the customer?* (problems solved or promised performance)
- *What image does it project?* (marketing strategy, advertising, and promotions)
- *What are potential objections and how can they be overcome?* (identify possible objections; prepare responses)

Have Empathy with the Customer. Empathy is the ability to see a situation through a customer's point of view. Almost all successful salespeople are sensitive to a customer's concerns, objections, fears, and feelings; they sincerely understand the customer's point of view. This understanding allows objections to be addressed and barriers to be broken down. The attitude that a sale is just a way to make money inevitably fails.

Set Goals. Like many other goals in life, to succeed, you must assist others (your client) in succeeding. Stay focused on your client's success, and your own success will follow.

Success starts with clear expectations, and solid, specific written goals. In goal setting, remember to:

- State expectations in measurable terms.
- Make yourself stretch to meet goals.
- State expectations as specific results. For example:

  Not: "Increase customers."

  But: "Win four new customers in October."

Set expectations beyond your comfort level. Giving an extra 10 percent effort toward your goals can make a difference that will reward you many times over.

Create and Follow a Solid Work Plan. Here are some tips to increase your success in business development.

- Make more contacts with prospective customers.
- Do more research before holding meetings.
- Prepare for and schedule more face-to-face meetings.
- Be professional.
- Be pleasant yet persistent.
- Don't take rejection personally.

If you want to drive from Florida to California, you get out a map and plan the trip. The same is true for reaching your business development goal. Here's a plan to close two more new clients each month. Follow these five steps to increase your number of successful closes.

1. Make a specific number of additional sales calls each week.
2. Define the kind of prospects you will call on.

3. Plan how you will introduce yourself to those prospects and how you will prepare for the meetings.
4. Determine how far ahead you will have to schedule your time to accommodate the extra calls.
5. Follow through and make the calls.

Follow these four steps to earn more business from current clients.

1. Set a goal for the number of relationships you wish to expand.
2. Select which clients you will target for increased business development.
3. Plan your approach with each client.
4. Follow through and make the calls.

Be Prepared. Whether approaching a prospective customer or an established customer, always be fully prepared for meetings.

- Read the client's industry magazines.
- Search the Internet for news related to the client's field.
- View the client's web page, annual report, and sales literature.
- Craft questions that show your knowledge and uncover client needs.
- Don't steal time.
- Set meetings only when you have a reason.
- Prepare in advance.
- Don't expect the customer to do your work for you.
- Be competent and mature.
- Make sure to take matters seriously and come across professionally.
- Don't aim to impress.
- Aim to make a good impression.

How to Develop Leads

It's impossible to present a product to everyone, so it's critical for business development to *prospect* or look for potential customers who:

- Have a particularly strong need for your product
- Have adequate resources to pay for your product
- Can be reached conveniently or efficiently

When prospecting, keep in mind:

- What you're selling
- Who the logical users of the product are
- The marketing plan to reach the prospects

One of the most effective ways to expand your client list is through referrals. *Always ask for referrals.*

Where do referrals come from? They come from customers, friends, business associates, vendors, family members, the marketing department, and so on. Referrals are your most likely source of new business. Don't let a single referral fall through the cracks. *Always follow up.*

To start finding contacts by *networking* with friends and business contacts, try these ideas:

- Chamber of Commerce
- Service clubs
- Civic groups
- Church groups

Also, stay in touch with former employers and employee associates. Tap into the far-reaching network of suppliers and vendors, and seek advice from other businesspeople, such as your attorney, accountant, and other acquaintances who are managers or small business owners.

In *sector prospecting*, you look for customers of a certain size or within a particular business segment. To do sector prospecting, check out the:

- Yellow pages
- Chamber of Commerce directories
- Local, regional, or state economic development directories
- Internet listings
- Key industry business directories published by local newspapers

Community prospecting groups:

- Consist of members from several business sectors with knowledge about the region's business environment.
- Meet weekly or monthly to discuss business development opportunities.
- Structure the group so that competitors don't attend the same meeting.
- Give and receive advice and assistance in making initial calls on prospects.
- Stay abreast of new businesses coming to your community.
- Learn about opportunities in existing businesses before they break in the general news.
- Discuss techniques and ideas to assist in your business development effort.

A *cold call* is a visit or phone call to a prospect you don't know and who is not expecting to hear from you. Always do your best to warm things up. Work through your network to pave the way to your first appointment by having an associate call the prospect in advance or by using an associate's name as a door-opener whenever possible.

Another technique is to use in-person cold calls as *research visits*. Go into an in-person cold call with a friendly face. Greet the receptionist or front-office staff professionally and warmly. Ask for general information and identify your industry without drawing attention to your interest in a sale. Say, for example, "I'm in banking." Obtain literature if available. Ask: "Do you have a corporate brochure?"

The close of your session with the receptionist or front-office staff depends on how the overall visit with him or her went.

If it went well, say something like this to the receptionist or front-office staff: "Here's my card. Thank you for your help. I'll be calling back for an appointment."

If it didn't go well, don't leave a card with the receptionist or front-office staff. Just say, "Thanks for your time."

Unless you have a photographic memory, take notes the moment you get outside the door, including:

- The name of the person you spoke with
- Information about the nature of the business
- Observations you made about the company while standing in the offices

Every time you make a call you risk hearing the word "no." Selling is a game of percentages. It's a fact: You are going to hear the word "no." But a "no" doesn't mean you've erred. It means, instead, that the prospect just doesn't want or need what you are selling at the moment. The law of probability predicts that every "no" moves you one step closer to the next "yes." Increase your presentations to increase your "nos" to increase your "yeses."

Introductory Call or Letter

There are various ways to secure a meeting with a prospect. Using a referral call or letter greatly increases your chances of obtaining a face-to-face meeting. When you do obtain your goal of a meeting with a decision maker, it is important to touch base and confirm prior to the meeting.

Getting a Meeting with a Prospect

There are several ways to attempt to get a meeting with a prospect:

- Cold calls (discussed earlier)
- Chance meetings
- Written requests
- Referral calls

Cold Calls

- A long shot
- Most appropriate for low-involvement purchases
- *Not* appropriate for important decisions, such as selecting a banking partner, an insurance policy, or other financial choices

Chance Meetings

- Don't count on chance meetings to deliver business opportunities.
- Take advantage of them when they arise.
- Be careful to keep the exchange appropriate to the casual tone of the meeting ground.

Written Requests

- Make an introduction.
- Request an appointment.
- Good letters leave a lasting impression.

Referral Calls

- Introduce yourself as a referral.
- Aim to schedule a first meeting.

Phone Rules

Getting through to a decision maker is like finding your way through a maze. Your success often depends on your ability to make an ally out of the person screening the decision maker's calls.

Be friendly, professional, and forthright. If a receptionist or assistant answers:

- Explain why you are calling.
- Ask for assistance.
- If the person is unavailable, ask when would be a good time to call back.
- Avoid secrecy.
- Work to form a partnership with the intermediary on the other end of the line. Keep it short, clear, and pleasant.
- Don't go into a sales pitch.
- Be professional but personable.
- Ask for the appointment, not the sale.
- Don't try to give a sales pitch over the phone.
- Make a good impression.
- Emphasize the value of the product.
- Quit talking and sign off.

Keep calling.

- Don't expect your call to be returned.
- Decision makers turn to pressing business first, and your call probably isn't in that pile.
- Try calling early and late, when your call might slip through.

When you reach the decision-maker, this is what you need to do during the call:

- Introduce yourself and your company, using a referral if possible.

- Converse in a manner that makes the decision maker want to meet with you in person.
- Explain the reason for your call so that the decision maker quickly knows what's in it for him or her.
- Use an assumptive approach by politely assuming that the prospect will agree to a meeting.
- State how much time you need and when you are hoping to meet.

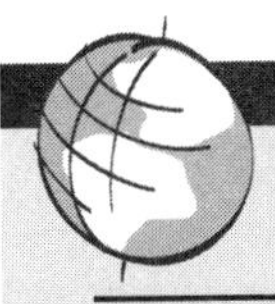

IN THE REAL WORLD

Sample Script

Self-introduction 	"Ms. Jones, this is Ann Smith with ABC Bank."
Use of referral 	"One of our customers is Diane Brown of Shoes and More, and she suggested we meet. Perhaps she's already mentioned my name to you."
Customer benefit	"We have a new banking package for businesses that saves money and earns interest while improving your banking service."
Assumptive approach 	"I know you're very busy right now. I'd like to set a 20-minute meeting to explore the possibilities....Would later this week be convenient, or would you prefer early next week?"

Sample Script: Dealing with Objections

Be ready with responses when the prospect hesitates or objects.

Prospect reply . . .	Your response . . .
"I'm very busy now, but could we talk about it another time?"	"Great. Is morning or afternoon best for you? Would 2:00 this Thursday work for you?"

In the Real World (continued)

"I'm very satisfied with my bank and don't see any reason to consider a change."		"I understand how you feel. If your bank is meeting your needs, I don't recommend a change. However, I'd like you to know about our unique business accounts and programs in case your situation changes. Is morning or afternoon best for you?"
"Could you send me a brochure?"		"Could I drop it off and take no more than 15 minutes to explain it and answer your questions? How would Thursday afternoon work?"

Confirmation of an Appointment

Confirm the appointment twice:

- *At the end of your phone conversation,* ensure agreement on day and time, ask if anyone else should attend the meeting, and give your phone number, in case a conflict arises.
- *Reconfirm one day before the meeting.* Reconfirming ensures you will not waste your time and demonstrates that you are an effective and well-organized businessperson who respects the value of time.

Putting Your Request in Writing

E-mail or a letter may be the best way to make a professional first impression when you can't get through in person or on the phone.

Tips and Techniques

Don't focus on yourself.	Focus on the prospect. Explain how your product will help his or her situation.

TIPS AND TECHNIQUES (CONTINUED)

Introduce yourself in terms that matter to the reader.	Reference the meeting, if you've met. Say who referred you. Avoid "I" statements. Instead, say: "It was great to meet you at Rotary." "We have a mutual friend in John Black."
State customer benefits.	Give benefits, not features. Cite facts to prove your point and show an understanding of the prospect's business.
Keep it short.	Fit it on one page.
What's your point?	Say thank you or make your request clearly: "I will call you early next week to schedule a time to meet."
Proofread carefully.	Ask someone else to read your letter. Don't send it until you've read it over one last time.

Always, double-check the spelling of the prospect's name and address.

Analyzing Client Needs

A *needs-analysis meeting* must reveal your prospect's needs. Your responsibility is to do your homework so that you're ready to focus the meeting and understand the information the prospect gives.

The kinds of questions you ask and your follow-up probing will determine your success in gathering the information you need to develop a winning proposal.

Conducting an assessment of a prospective client's situation is one of the most important steps in business development. The needs analysis allows you to determine the prospect's need for your product.

Information from a needs analysis allows you to tailor your offering to the prospect's unique situation. The needs analysis will help you to develop a personalized presentation later. Prospects are more likely to say "yes" to a presentation that is oriented to their unique circumstances and needs.

Planning the Meeting

The decision maker is a busy person who will give time for your interview only if it is of clear benefit to his or her business situation. Prepare yourself for the meeting by doing your homework in advance.

Tips and Techniques

Do Your Homework

Read:	The company's printed and online information
	News articles on the business and its industry
Consult your network:	Who's who in the prospect's organization
	The business's performance
	The business's competitive situation
Look for common interests with the decision maker:	Personality
	Lifestyle interests

Always consider past client relationships. Has the prospect's organization done business with your organization in the past? If so, review the entire client relationship before the meeting. Then approach the prospect as if he or she is already a client. *Nothing makes a past customer feel less important than being treated like a stranger.*

The needs-analysis meeting must give you the information you need to develop a proposal that will cause prospects to:

- Identify their own need.
- Recognize that your product can meet that need.
- Choose your product because it delivers value that justifies the price.

Needs-Analysis Interview

The more the prospect talks, the more likely a sale is to occur.

Too many salespeople launch into sales instead of taking time to listen to the prospect's needs. Ask questions that require explanation. Avoid "Do you . . ." and "Are you . . ." questions that can be answered with a simple nod. "Who," "What," "When," "Where," "Why," and "How" and "Tell me . . ." questions lead to dialog, give the prospect a chance to brag a little, and demonstrate you've done your homework. Let the prospect talk without interruptions, and make a mental note when a point needs clarification.

There is always the chance that the prospect will make the choice to do business with you during the needs-analysis meeting. But don't count on it! Don't be the one to convert your information-gathering meeting into a sales presentation.

Remember, this is a fact-finding call:

- Don't make sales points about your organization.
- You are there to find out more about your prospect's business.
- Briefly introduce yourself and your business.
- Answer specific client questions about a particular service or aspect of your offering, but be brief.
- Save the selling for the next call.

A needs-analysis meeting should include three general steps:

1. Brief introduction
2. How your company's expertise relates to the prospect's business
3. Transition to questions

IN THE REAL WORLD

Sample Script

Brief introduction:	"As I mentioned last week on the phone, The Bank of Florida has been in the community for 25 years."
Relate to the prospect:	"We specialize in serving as a strong banking partner for small- to medium-size businesses, and we've helped many regional firms like yours improve their banking services. I believe we can do the same for your business."
Transition to questions:	"In order to tailor our programs to your unique needs, I would to like to spend a few minutes obtaining an overview of your firm and its needs."
Sample Questions	
Tell me	"Mr. Smith, tell me about your business." "Tell me what services you currently receive that you like."
What, when, where, how Move from general topics to more focused questions as the interview proceeds and confidence is established.	"Where are you banking at this time?" "What, in your opinion, could they do better or what do they not offer?" "I know you started in 1982, and I'm aware of many of your customers, but how do you describe your clients and why you are successful?" "What other banking needs do you have that we haven't discussed? Is there anything else you'd like me to know about your banking requirements so that I can tailor our proposal to your needs?"

You need to do follow-up probing to get the information you need and to clarify what the prospect's answers mean.

Probing Tips

- Listen to the prospect's comment before probing further.
- Keep your tone conversational—as if you're working together with the prospect on a solution.
- Remember you are fact-gathering, not interrogating or even selling.

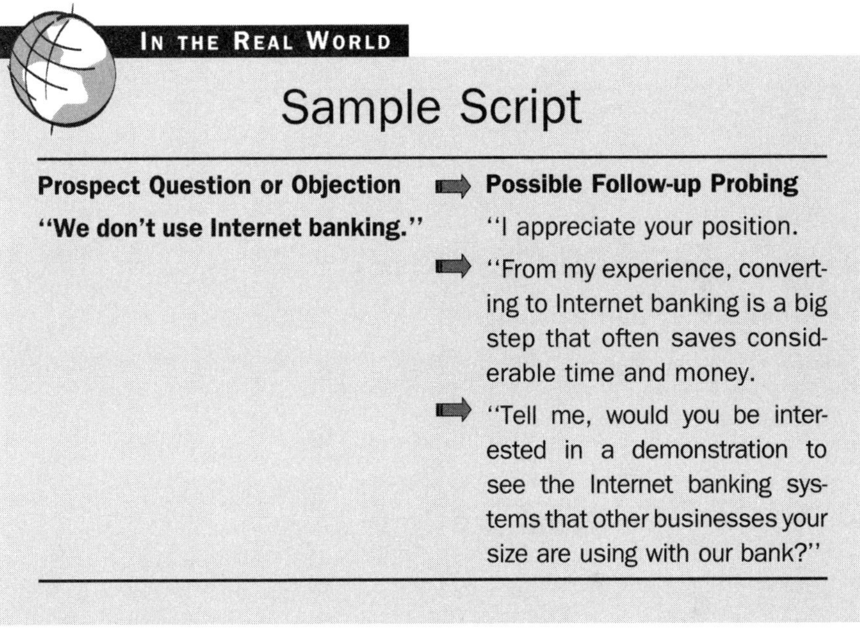

IN THE REAL WORLD

Sample Script

Prospect Question or Objection	Possible Follow-up Probing
"We don't use Internet banking."	"I appreciate your position.
	"From my experience, converting to Internet banking is a big step that often saves considerable time and money.
	"Tell me, would you be interested in a demonstration to see the Internet banking systems that other businesses your size are using with our bank?"

As you wind up your interview, it is often helpful to summarize the conversation to make sure you've heard the answers correctly and to allow the prospect to provide additional information that will be useful to your proposal. You should:

- Restate
- Invite input
- Move on

IN THE REAL WORLD

Sample Script

Restate: "So, Mr. Smith, what I hear you saying is that your major needs may include a revolving line of credit to draw on when needed, a program to save time and money with Internet banking, and perhaps more responsive overall service from your bank."

Invite input: "Did I miss anything that you would like us to address?"

Move on: "We will prepare our proposal based on the needs you have expressed."

As you bring the needs-analysis meeting to an end, be sure to:

- Thank the prospect for his or her time.
- Advise what your next step is.
- Set the next meeting.
- Conclude the meeting.

Preparing the Presentation

It's important to keep the purpose of the meeting in mind when developing your presentation. Use information from the needs-analysis meeting to focus the presentation on how your product or service uniquely meets the prospect's needs.

The presentation is the opportunity to present your proposal, product, or concept in person; to summarize key selling points; to respond to questions and concerns; and to explain benefits directly to the prospective decision makers and influencers.

If done correctly, the needs-analysis meeting provides the information needed to prepare the presentation. The presentation must:

- *Make a good impression.* Convince prospects that you and your organization are the ones with whom they want to work.
- *Describe the benefits of your product.* Use an easy-to-understand style that explains your product in terms of what the prospects want and need.
- *Ask for the order.* Emphasize the value of your product as you ask for the order.

Elements of the Presentation

You are the main feature of the in-person presentation, but you'll need to use some other tools to supplement your speaking points. These tools include:

- A written summary
- Audiovisual support materials
- Demonstrations
- Testimonials

Putting your case in writing assures that your client can refer back to your sales points as he or she considers your proposal.

Decide exactly what you are trying to prove:

- What claim you are trying to make
- Why that claim is important to the prospect's success

Describe your product:

- Features
- Benefits
- Value for cost

Present the strengths of your organization:

- Reliability
- Trustworthiness as a business partner

Before you prepare the final version of the presentation, ask a colleague to look over any written material you will present to a prospect.

Presentation Day

If you want to keep the attention of the audience, go through the main points in person before passing out a written summary. You can advise the audience that they will receive a copy after the meeting.

The benefits of PowerPoint slides or other visual support materials are that they:

- Focus attention on the key points you are making.
- Provide visual prompts, reducing reliance on notes and contributing to your confidence level.

Visual materials should be:

- Straightforward and simple
- Free of typos or grammatical mistakes
- Entertaining and impressive, if possible

Whenever possible, let your product speak for itself. Show how it works through demonstrations that allow your prospects to:

- Touch your product
- Try it themselves
- Hold it in their own hands

When prospects participate in a demonstration, their use of the new product reduces resistance to change.

Be sure you are the best person to demonstrate the product. Bring along an expert if you're not 100 percent sure how it works or how to answer questions that might arise.

Testimonials are statements, usually written, in support of facts or truths leading to an affirmation of your business's character or worth.

Testimonials add to your credibility. Evidence that your organization's products and services have worked effectively for other businesses can give the prospect confidence in your company.

Make sure the testimonial relates to benefits that the prospect cares about. A testimonial from a customer who values the prestige of your organization won't help sell a prospect who is seeking cost efficiencies from the most economical service provider.

Use the Prospect's Language

Avoid using technical jargon. Keep your language conversational. Make the prospect comfortable and increase his or her confidence in your ability to understand and relate to his or her business environment.

Remember, people buy benefits, not features. Discover benefits your product will deliver and present those as selling points.

Feature	Benefit
"Our bank has a new Internet program so you can pay all of your monthly creditors electronically."	"You can save time and money while you manage cash flow more efficiently by using our easy and convenient Internet program to pay your creditors electronically."

Setting the Presentation Date and Time

Setting the presentation date and time is a critical step in the business development process. You need to:

- *State how much time is needed.* With this information, the prospect can set aside an uninterrupted block of time.

- *Be ready to counter a request that you merely drop off the proposal.* Politely explain the benefit of allowing you to explain key points and respond to questions or ideas.
- *Verify who will attend the presentation.* Do this to:
  - Bring the right number of handouts.
  - Ensure the decision maker will be there.
  - Prepare for the audience.
- *Plan for necessary audiovisual equipment.*
  - Confirm that the room is appropriate for your needs.
  - Offer to discuss these needs with an administrative assistant out of regard for the decision maker's time.

Making the Presentation

When making a presentation, it is important to put the prospect at ease, present a positive image of your company, and make the prospect part of the presentation by asking appropriate questions.

Remember, it's important to emphasize the benefits of your product or service, not the features. Proving the effectiveness of the product or service in meeting the prospect's needs is the surest way to catch his or her attention.

Effective discussions of cost will compare the price to the value that your product or service delivers.

Take a few minutes to factually present the compelling strengths of your organization. Make the prospect part of the presentation:

- Keep your presentation conversational by talking *with* the decision maker, not *to* him or her.
- Periodically ask questions to determine interest.

Sample Presentation Script

Follow the sequence in this script to ensure your presentation is effective.

Sample Script

Present the product/service:	➡	"Mr. Smith, with our new Internet program you can pay all of your creditors electronically."
Describe the benefit:	➡	"What this means to you is that your company can save time and money each month."
Prove effectiveness:	➡	"We have many clients who tell us that they have saved up to 50 percent of the cost of bill paying compared to using checks."
Involve the prospect:	➡	"How frequently do you currently issue checks?"

Discussing Cost

No one wants to spend money. It is your job to move the focus from what your product *costs* to the value it *delivers*. Concentrate on what will be *gained* in return for the purchasing decision, not on the dollars it costs.

Don't be afraid to state the cost of your product. The customer needs to know, and you shouldn't hesitate to explain pricing. Be confident that the price is low compared to the resulting value. Move right on to value. Show how your product has the potential to:

- Increase business.
- Save operating costs.
- Improve customer service and/or employee satisfaction.
- Deliver value in excess of the product's price.

Use the difference between price and value when making cost comparisons.

- Present a cost comparison between the price and value of your product.
- Compare your price to that of your competitors.

Your product may offer an excellent benefit based on price alone, but if your cost is higher than your competitors', present intangible benefits showing higher value to justify your higher price, including:

- Extraordinary level of service
- Service guarantees
- Unchallenged safety, quality, or other characteristics

Ultimately, people choose to do business with people whom they like and trust. Keep these truths in mind:

- The best policy for sales is to be straightforward and focus on the client's best interest.
- Unachievable expectations will hurt your business in the long run.
- You risk misleading the prospect and endangering his or her trust if you guess at answers rather than researching before responding.

Closing the Sale

To be successful, you must approach the prospect assuming that he or she will buy. In this process, called "the assumptive sales process," statements, questions, and plans for the meeting all reflect your belief that the prospect wants to buy.

It is important to recognize buying signals and to act on them. Likewise, in the absence of buying signals, it is important to pose a question as a trial close. Also, there are specific methods to overcome objections and to close a sale smoothly.

Once the buying decision is made, it is important to summarize the decision and present the next steps. This section specifically addresses:

- The assumptive sale
- Buying signals
- The close

- After the buying decision: summary and review
- Future closing
- Objections

Assumptive Sale

Assume that the prospect will buy. Throughout your presentation, pose your statements and questions as if the prospect wants to buy your product or service.

Plan for closing the sale: If you know in advance how you plan to ask for the customer's business, your success rate will be much higher.

Assumptive Statements	Nonassumptive Statements
Ms. Smith, as a customer of our bank . . .	Ms. Smith, if you decide to do business with us . . .

Your confident attitude:

- Removes doubt from the prospect's mind.
- Increases the chance of a positive buying decision.

Buying Signals

A "buying signal" is a subtle clue indicating that the decision maker is relaxed and interested in what you are offering. The prospect is transmitting buying signals when he or she:

- Asks questions.
  - "Could I see that again?"
  - "Can the program be customized?"
  - "Could I get an automatic sweep account with your bank?"

- Clearly agrees with you.
  - Nods.
  - Shows enthusiasm about your offering.
- Visibly relaxes.
  - Answers questions quickly and comfortably.
- Shows positive actions.
  - Leans forward.
  - Makes more eye contact.
  - Handles the sales literature.
  - Makes calculations while you're talking.

A succession of buying signals tells you to stop selling and to ask for the order.

The Close

"Closing" is defined as asking for the order.

Sample Closing Script

Answer the question:	➡	"Yes, Mr. Williams, we do have an automatic sweep account."
Use an assumptive close:	➡	"Shall we plan on using that feature for your business?"
If client agrees:	➡	"Would you like to switch your accounts now or wait until the first of the month?"
If client disagrees:	➡	"What other questions do you have about doing business with our bank?"

Trial Close. What if there's no clear buying signal?

Up to two-thirds of all sales presentations come to an end without the salesperson asking for the order. If there are no clear buying signals, consider using a trial closing.

Sample Trial Close Script

Pose a question:	➡	"Mr. Williams, on your revolving credit line, how much each year do you feel you would need?"
Move to the close:	➡	"Great."
Be assumptive:	➡	"Then shall we submit that amount on the application?"

Remember to ask and listen.

If you find yourself doing all of the talking, the prospect has not been engaged and your chances of making the sale will be lower.

Summary Close. Another way to close your presentation is to summarize your main points and simply ask for the order.

Sample Summary Close Script

Summarize:	➡	"Mr. Williams, we've discussed how our bank will handle your loan needs, your checking accounts, your use of the Internet, and other needs you may have."
Prompt dialog:	➡	"Are there any other areas that you have questions about?"
If prospect has questions:	➡	(Provide answers.)
If prospect does not have questions:	➡	(Ask for the order.)

After the Buying Decision: Summary and Review

Once you've arrived at a positive buying decision, you are no longer talking with a prospect. Now you're meeting with a client. Move immediately into a discussion of the details of setting up client accounts and explain the next steps you will be taking together to establish your business relationship.

Future Closing

Often the prospect needs more time before making a buying decision. If the prospect needs more time, you should:

- Ask for a specific time to meet again, aiming for a date in the near future.
- Remember that the more time that passes, the more apt the prospect is to forget about your proposal.

TIPS AND TECHNIQUES

Don't Give Up Too Soon

Studies show that more than half of all customers say "no" four times before they say "yes." Yet most salespeople quit asking for the order after the first or second time that they hear "no." Often "no" means "not yet."

Don't quit. And at the same time, don't become a broken record or an arm-twister.

Instead, find another way to meet the prospect's needs, work to overcome objections, move the prospect to a buying signal, and then ask—again—for the order.

Objections

People avoid decisions and generally dislike change. As a result, they come up with objections to defer saying "yes" to a new proposal. When prospects say:

"We're already very satisfied."

"The timing isn't right."

"I'm not sure your bank is for me."

. . . nod your head, acknowledge their point of view, rephrase and repeat, ask questions, establish rapport, and stay calm. Then, gently, explain the value of your product in terms that counter the objection.

Seek a point of agreement. Acknowledge and confirm the objections, and then move on to explain how your product addresses the need and overcomes the objection. Respond: "I see what you're saying . . .." Then continue discussing the benefits of what your bank offers.

- Don't get defensive.
- Positively respond to the prospect's objection with a strong point that overcomes the objection.
- Present the benefit.
- Move every response into a presentation of how the prospect will benefit from a positive decision.

Every now and then you'll run into a prospect with an endless list of objections. Reasons may include:

- The prospect is skirting around an awkward objection that he or she is hesitant to mention.
- The prospect may not be interested in buying at all.

In the case of an unstated objection, say something like: "Mr. Williams, I want to address all your concerns, but are these objections your real concern, or is there another issue you'd like us to discuss?"

Check the prospect's interest in buying. Ask: "If I can address this issue to your satisfaction, would you be willing to move your accounts to our bank?"

When you've answered the final objection, stop talking. In the silence that follows, your instinct will be to talk some more. *Don't!* The prospect will also want to end the silence, so wait and let him or her do the talking. The next word you hear could be "yes."

Follow-up and Service

Once you've closed the sale, some of the banker's most important work begins: showing appreciation to the customer and working to keep him or her happy. Customer service gives the business development banker the opportunity to make a client a customer for life.

Follow-up and service is the responsibility of the business development professional. It is far easier and less expensive for the banker charged with business development to keep an existing customer happy than for him or her to develop a new customer. Send a thank-you note immediately after the presentation.

- Follow up with an immaculately neat letter outlining the major points of your agreement.
- Invite the customer to functions or find other ways to show that you enjoy the customer's company and appreciate his or her business.

Aim to make the customer a customer for life.

Summary

Business development encompasses all phases of the marketing process, from identifying the prospect to closing the sale and establishing the customer relationship. In banking, the role of business development is to make the sale. Business development takes the marketing message to prospect, presents the product as a solution to the prospect's needs, and wins the business, thereby establishing the client relationship. Marketing is different from business development in that marketing represents the big picture, or the strategic process of planning and executing the conception, pricing, promotion, and distribution of ideas, goods, and services, whereas business development represents the frontline effort.

There are several steps in the business development cycle. You must know your product, including its features and how it is different from competing products, the reason it was developed, who developed it, and what problems it solves. You must also understand the possible objections your prospect might have and what the appropriate repsonse to these objections might be. It is also useful to understand the product's marketing strategy and plans for advertising and and promotions.

You must be prepared for the sale physically and mentally. This means that in addition to knowing your product, you must set goals, create and follow a work plan, dress professionally for prospect meetings, and be prepared for the unknown.

It is critical to develop leads and prospect for new customers. Lead development might include cold calls, getting referrals, networking, community outreach, sector prospecting, and other sources. Learning to warm up cold calls and getting beyond the "no" to sell an appointment are valuable skills to assist in developing leads. For example, one way of warming up a cold call is to use cold calls as research visits. Another technique is the introductory letter, phone call, or e-mail.

An important responsibility for the business development professional is analyzing prospect needs. This allows him or her to match requirements against bank products and services. Needs analysis requires a considerable amount of probing and even more listening. Information from the needs analysis will help focus the sales presentation on how the product or service uniquely meets the prospect's needs. The presentation may include a demonstration of the product. When prospects participate in a demonstration, often their resistance to change is reduced. This is especially true when they can touch the product or try it themselves.

Closing the sale always calls for a call to action. An effective technique is the assumptive sale. In an assumptive sale, your statements, questions, and plans for the meeting all reflect your belief that the prospect wants to buy.

Once the sale is closed, be attentive to and appreciative of the customer's business. Keep in touch with the customer on a regular basis with the intention of creating a lifelong customer.

CHAPTER 7

The Ethical Banker: An Introduction to Ethics

After reading this chapter, you will be able to:

- Explain why it is important to study ethics.
- Understand how professionals develop ethical behavior.
- Discuss what is unique about ethics and banking.
- Describe the responsibilities of an ethical banker.

Beyond sales strategies and marketing savvy, the profession of the banker, unlike many others, is one for which people carry an elevated expectation of ethical standards.

We all know, and common sense dictates, that an ethical professional is one who operates from a strong sense of right and wrong and possesses an unrelenting commitment to doing the right thing, especially in situations not explicitly addressed in codes of conduct.

But what makes an ethical banker, and how is the expectation of ethics in banking different from other businesses? How does one obtain a "code of ethics"? Is it learned? Inherited? Part of an individual's unique genetic makeup? This chapter will help you to answer these questions and more.

What Is "Ethics"?

Ethics is the practice of applying ideas of right and wrong to create and uphold codes of behavior that help guide people. An ethical professional:

- Follows the rules of fair and responsible conduct in his or her profession.
- Exercises independent judgment to do the right thing, especially in situations not explicitly addressed in codes of conduct.

While many people believe that adopting a formal code of ethics is not important, you may be surprised to learn that the formal study of ethics is necessary. Becoming an ethical professional involves study, learning new behaviors, and developing unique skills. Ethical professionals generally build relationships of trust and demonstrate courageous behaviors when their ethics are tested.

What is unique about banking and ethics? Is it enough that decent people will do the right thing? Being trusted with people's money carries a special burden. Bankers are entrusted with people's futures: education of children, retirement, and quality of life.

That trust places a special burden on bankers to understand the ethics of the roles they play and to do the right thing every time. The study of ethics is important to enable bankers to do the right thing all of the time. It's simply not enough to offer good advice and service to 99 percent of the people who seek aid.

New investment challenges emphasize ethics. The study of ethics will help in facing new situations due to the:

- Emergence of new financial instruments
- Quickening pace of globalization of the markets
- Increasing role of technology in people's financial lives

Every professional situation in banking involves a number of key players. The first step toward the ethical practice of the profession is an ongoing awareness of how every act the banker performs affects each of these parties:

- Individual banker
- Customer
- Institution
- Public

The Individual Banker

"Following orders" is never an acceptable excuse for taking unethical actions. You need to be sure that you don't bend or break your personal standards of right and wrong in the course of your work.

You always personally bear responsibility for your actions, regardless of who tells you what you do or your reason for doing it. Ignorance of ethical standards is not acceptable, either. You have an affirmative obligation to learn about the ethical standards of your profession, your employer, and the regulatory bodies that govern the work you do.

Most professional associations in the financial services industry have codes of ethics that are required for membership. Violation of the code results in stripping the member of his or her rights, credentials, and privileges afforded by the organization.

The Customer

Your customer, often called the "account holder," is the individual or institution to whom you provide your products and services. In order to ethically serve your customers, your information needs to be more than just truthful. You need to understand your client's current and future financial needs and be sure that the advice and service you offer is appropriate for the customer.

The Institution

One of the parties your actions impact most is your employer, the banking institution. This is one of the reasons why you must earn the trust you are given while operating within the bounds of your agreements with your employer. You must fairly represent the bank you work for in any and all of your day-to-day activities. The people with whom you work will have a direct impact on your ability to carry out your duties in a professional and forthright manner. You need to contribute to the creation and sustenance of an ethical organization by sharing and sticking to standards of appropriate behavior and creating opportunities for the people you work with to challenge your ethical behavior and that of your institution.

The Public

The public's trust of bankers contributes to the stability of U.S. financial markets, thus allowing people to confidently:

- Invest for their future security.
- Borrow funds for making their dreams become reality here and now.

When the public's trust of bankers is violated, a chip is taken out of the wall of stability in capital markets. Every professional action you take has ethical significance that extends from your relationship to your client and from your institution to the public's trust in U.S. financial markets.

Ethical Obligations

Good Faith

An important challenge: As a banker, you must always act in good faith.

To act in good faith means that you must always let your customer know about any personal interest you have in advice given, even though you're sure that the advice will make money for him or her. You must also advise a client against action that might help you or your firm but isn't best for him or her.

Test your motivation by asking yourself how your advice would be viewed by others if your customer suffered the worst possible outcome of a decision you helped him or her reach. Your good faith would be questioned if anyone looking into the matter suspected you were motivated by something other than helping your client.

Responsibilities to the Client

As a banker, you have ethical obligations to clients seeking advice and service because the results can dramatically affect their lives. Some of the most important duties to clients remain:

- Putting the client's financial interest above your own interest or the interest of your employer or institution
- Ensuring a full disclosure of all the risks involved in any action, investment, or decision made
- Providing competent, fully informed advice and service
- Providing appropriate confidentiality
- Supplying written documentation of any transaction or agreement

Confidentiality is one of the more clear-cut ethical issues you'll face. As a banker, people share information with you that they often withhold from even their closest relatives. This information might involve:

- Income
- Debt
- Financial obligations

You enjoy a special relationship when people share financial information with you. In some states, you are even protected from testifying or sharing information about your clients with police, because the government recognizes a special connection between people and their financial counselors.

Bankers must take these precautions to maintain a client's confidentiality:

- Avoid chatting with friends about clients' finances.
- Keep your records properly protected: lock and key for paper files and appropriate firewalls and other electronic security measures for records kept on computers.

Most bankers feel that ethical practice demands that access to information be restricted even within their own organizations. Restricted access requires decisions regarding:

- Who has access to clients' financial records
- How to respond to client requests to follow the same investment advice given to another customer
- How to respond to requests from mailing-list and lead-sheet operations to buy names of your clients in order to solicit business from them

Many bankers make decisions about who should have access to restricted client files based on who has a real need to know. The need-to-know standard requires a system to ensure the security of customer files and makes sharing information about clients with other clients clearly off limits.

Selling or sharing information with third parties is a common practice in some corners of the banking industry while it is entirely taboo in others. You'll never go wrong if you share information about a client only after asking for his or her permission.

You need to share documentation of all transactions or agreements with each customer. Good service requires that you provide a written record. Documentation protects both parties by ensuring a meeting of the minds that helps you both to be sure of what you've agreed to. By providing a clear paper trail of clients' financial lives, you facilitate self-management of their business, which makes them less dependent on you.

Responsibilities to Others

Most bankers are part of a larger organization and do not work as independent contractors. But as a banker, you also have:

- Important relationships with the companies whose products you sell, recommend, or evaluate
- Special obligations, to the public at large, that extend beyond your obligations to your individual client

You have ethical obligations to your employer that may be:

- Spelled out in an employment contract or employee handbook
- Important but not written down anywhere

Ethical obligations range from easily attainable job performance standards to more challenging behaviors. Here is the range of ethical obligations that you as an employee have to your employer:

- Show up on time.
- Put in a full day's work.
- Participate in ongoing training.
- Make a personal commitment to work up to your abilities.
- Speak up when you see unethical behavior.

Your responsibilities don't stop with your employer—you also have responsibilities to the public. U.S. financial markets are the world standard for fairness, efficiency, and reliability.

As a banker, you have a special obligation to live up to the public's trust. What you do personally affects your clients' attitudes toward the financial markets generally, and those collective feelings have great significance for all of us.

Obligation to Learn and Be Forthright

Just as you have an obligation to your clients to be knowledgeable about the products and services you provide, as an employee, you also have an obligation to learn what you need to know to help fulfill the promises your employer makes to its customers.

Your competence is required to meet your employer's responsibility to the customer. Promises by your employer to provide expertise or services require you to make a good faith effort to learn what your role requires, even if those promises cover areas that don't appeal to you. If you are not able or willing to participate in some areas of your company's service, you must be honest and forthright with your employer. Your employer will need to work around your limitations while still delivering on the promises it made to clients.

All employees who act unethically victimize the companies they work for. An important obligation to an employer, and one that is often overlooked, is active objection to unethical behavior within your company.

If you work as part of an organization that is operating unethically in any way, your obligation is to:

- Object.
- Make your objections clear to management at as high a level as you can reach.

In many cases, your institution will reward you for your vigilance—but it may not. Even if your ethical objections cause you to have to leave your position, you are better off being true to your personal and professional standards than you would be if you made loyalty to an unethical institution or boss your highest priority.

Serious consequences result from failure to object to unethical practices. Certain bankers, some of whom were innocent bystanders who chose not to object to the unethical practices of their employers, are now banned from their professions because regulators caught on to the unethical acts.

Trust is everything to the banking industry. In the United States, we have managed to build an infrastructure of trust unparalleled in history. Think about the economic benefits of this trust. What if institutions were unable to make million- and billion-dollar deals with a simple telephone call because that trust was missing? Without trust:

- The efficiency of our markets would shrink.
- The available capital for business would wither.
- Many more people would be uninsured.
- Surviving family members would be bereft of financial support.

By and large, bankers have met their ethical obligations to the public year after year, decade after decade. Because of this, today, in the United States, ordinary citizens can pick up the phone and trade stocks with full trust in the brokers they deal with, even though they've never met them.

People walk into banks and hand hundreds or thousands of dollars to tellers and bank officers they might never have met before, with full faith that their funds will be credited to their account. As a banker, you bear a special burden of continuing that tradition of trust. When you uphold that trust, you encourage the fluidity of the financial markets.

Giving Back

There are no laws and few ethical codes that require anyone to serve their communities as volunteers or donors. Few will criticize a choice not to participate in community affairs, but playing an active role in your community and supporting worthy causes may result in praise and an increase in your stature as an ethical professional.

The Ethical Organization

"I'm a better banker because I do this," a Wall Street investment banker says as he spends a day building a new home in New York's Lower East Side neighborhood with Habitat for Humanity. Had he not volunteered, few would have accused him of an ethical lapse. But because he does volunteer, many view him as a more ethical professional.

Religious philosopher Reinhold Niebuhr once said, "Groups are less moral than individuals." Why? Although people may be individually responsible, when they become part of a group, they feel little or no responsibility for what others in their group do. An ethical professional must not tolerate others who lie, cheat, or steal.

How do you play a positive role in the ethical conduct of your organization? Although your role depends (in part) on your position, you can exert influence on others around you by:

- Example
- Persuasion
- Formal authority

A highly ethical organization begins with a clear vision and picture of integrity throughout the organization. Ethical principles require that:

- Management embodies the vision.
- Any reward system is aligned with the vision.
- External and internal policies are aligned with the vision.
- There is an understanding that every significant management decision has ethical value dimensions.

The most powerful tool you have for affecting the behavior of others is your own behavior. But if you want to influence the people you work with, you need to do more than adhere to your own standards. You need to let your colleagues know what those standards are. Where do your standards come from?

First, you need to be clear about the ethical standards you follow. Standards might come from a professional organization's code, your employer, personal commitments, or a combination of all of these.

Openly acknowledge the role of ethical standards in your actions. When you receive attention for work well done, mention the fact that you take these ethical standards seriously. The occasional reference to ethical standards will go a long way.

If you are asked to do something that you think is unethical, or if you become aware of unethical actions by others, make it clear to everyone involved that you won't violate the ethical standards and that you expect others around you to know and follow the ethics of your profession. If you know the specific ethical codes or principles that you think are at issue, bring them to the attention of your colleagues.

If you hold a management role in your organization, you have the opportunity to:

- Uphold ethical standards as you exercise formal authority.
- Integrate ethics with your current management practices.
- Create opportunities for employees to be involved in ethical decision making.

Corporate Blueprint for an Ethical Organization

The elements required to develop an ethical organization include:

- A code of ethics
- Ongoing training in professional ethics

- A clear and comfortable channel for expressing ethical concerns
- Outside ethics audits

Every organization should create, circulate, and regularly refer to a code of ethics that:

- Emphasizes adherence to laws and regulations
- Is a formal requirement of every job in your organization
- Reviews the traits necessary to enable the ethical and successful application of your product or service
- Identifies the values that produce behaviors exhibiting those traits

A structured communication of the Ethics Policies to all employees should be implemented as well as a regular, open review of the policies. The review should involve people from all levels of the organization.

Communication of ethics policies can be accomplished through ongoing training. The training in professional ethics should include a regular review of key concepts, discussions of the professional ethics involved in news reports relating to your organization's work, and review and discussion of ethical implications of case studies from your firm's work.

Challenge colleagues to make a concerted effort to raise the ethical quality of their work, emphasizing that everyone can always improve on the quality of their work habits.

An environment where employees and customers feel free to voice concerns is a critical element of an ethical organization. Furthermore, employees or clients who wish to challenge the ethics of actions taken on behalf of that organization must have easy access to a complaint process and be assured of anonymity.

Additionally, conduct outside ethics audits to highlight your commitment to maintaining an ethical organization. You need to be proactive in looking at the ethical state of your organization. The absence of complaints is not proof that all is well. On a regular basis, invite outsiders, including clients and colleagues, to take a look at the ways you do business from an ethical perspective.

Professional Code of Ethics

As a banker, you may belong to professional organizations. Some professions mandate membership in professional organizations, although in most professions it is usually voluntary. Members usually agree to follow a specific code of ethics.

Most codes of ethics:

- Set forth specific acts and attitudes required of members.
- Point out the fiduciary nature of client relationships.
- Prepare members to exercise independent judgment for those specific situations that no one can anticipate.
- Urge the professional to put the client's interest above his or her own.
- Require the professional to maintain reasonable standards of personal conduct outside and inside the office.

Some states and cities revoke licenses for breaches of professional codes, and some laws cite professional organizations' codes of ethics and require adherence to them. In civil suits, professionals may be found liable if their conduct does not follow the standards set by their professional organizations.

Codes of ethics serve as guideposts that require that you conduct yourself with integrity and honesty, avoid bad practices, and practice fairness and objectivity.

Codes of professional behavior (known as the *code of conduct*) relate to:

- Professional competence
- Behavior that enhances your profession and professional organization

- Compliance with all laws and regulations
- Adherence to your company's guidelines and policies
- Ethical action toward clients

Professional competence includes possession of the knowledge necessary to do a quality job, pursuing continuing education throughout your career, and recognizing and addressing your limitations.

Education and knowledge can make the difference between poorly prepared professionals who do a disservice to themselves and their clientele and true professionals who provide real service and value while protecting themselves from misrepresentation, incomplete disclosure, and general fiduciary liability.

Compliance with all laws and regulations is considered to be the minimum standard of acceptable behavior for professionals. This compliance must then be augmented with further ethical standards.

Codes of ethics usually require you to:

- Fulfill clients' needs with objectivity.
- Place their needs above your own.
- Maintain confidences and hold personal information in trust.
- Present all salient facts essential to your clients' decisions.

Good client relationships are critical for a successful banking career. Actions that may not be in your client's best interest may at times seem advantageous, but in the long run you can do no greater disservice to yourself than failing to provide the best possible service to your client.

Generic Corporate Codes of Ethics

Many corporations have their own formal codes of ethics—even though the code may not be widely circulated or discussed. Most such codes include some reference to these three important foundations of professional ethics: honesty, innovation, commitment.

These behaviors represent honesty:

- Trust one another to use sound judgment.
- The corporation makes every attempt to respect employee privacy.
- Be forthright.
- Fully disclose any pertinent information.
- Respect rights and property.
- Compete fairly.
- Keep accurate records.
- Exercise good judgment.

These behaviors represent innovation:

- Learn and create.
- Work together.
- Recruit, train, and promote based on performance.
- Encourage open communication.
- Give recognition.
- Value all employees without regard to level.
- Strive to win.
- Take responsible risks.
- Promote workplace flexibility.
- Recognize that we succeed or fail together.

These behaviors represent commitment:

- Take responsibility.
- Keep skills current.
- Create a positive workplace.
- Assume personal accountability.
- Protect the corporate reputation.

- Value open and fair competition.
- Abide by the letter and spirit of codes of conduct (behavior) and rules of business.
- Protect the corporation's assets.

Responding to Unethical Behavior

While many codes of ethics clearly guide your ethical behavior, few explain what action to take when you observe unethical behavior by someone else.

How should you respond if you feel a colleague has done something wrong and no one seems to care? Or if a colleague, client, or vendor has done something wrong, and won't acknowledge and remedy the act?

As an individual, you have the responsibility to act if you see someone else at your bank perform an unethical act or over the course of time adopt habits or ways of working that become unethical. You should take the next steps in the order listed. At each step, if the person does not take action to correct the unethical behavior, you proceed to the next step.

1. Tell your colleague how you feel.
2. Tell the person in your bank responsible for human resources/ethical complaints.
3. Tell the most senior person in your bank that you can contact.
4. Notify any professional association to which your colleague belongs.

Doing the right thing is not always easy. When you bring up the topic of unethical behavior in your company, you're testing your company's ethics to a degree. In some organizations, the unfortunate truth is that your vigilance will be held against you. The ethical path is clear: Keeping silent about a colleague's or superior's unethical behavior in order to protect yourself is, in fact, unethical.

If you are in a position to shape your organization's policies, take these actions:

- Make all of your colleagues feel comfortable in challenging the ethics of any action or advice that anyone at your bank delivers.
- Appoint an ethics officer who regularly seeks out opinions about the ethical standards at your bank and is available to take anonymous ethics complaints.
- Ensure that the process of dealing with ethics complaints is entirely separate from your bank's regular human resources activities.
- Protect employees from unfair retribution for reporting concerns about ethical issues.

Why are ethics important? From a social perspective, ethical behavior makes our communities better places to live. Our lives, and the lives of our families, are undeniably better when every individual plays by the rules.

Ethical behavior is not about what's in it for you. The only enduring reason to do the right thing is that it's right. If you earn a reputation as being an ethical professional, you'll probably have a better career and a happier life.

You've examined ethical situations that were clearly defined. This section gives you guidance to make ethical decisions when situations fall into gray areas where specific conduct is not necessarily expected or addressed. It shows how common sense and a basic understanding of proper ethical conduct gives you the tools to deal with sticky ethical situations.

Not all situations present obvious ethical choices, such as whether to lie, steal, cheat, abuse another, or break the terms of a contract. Your real-life ethical dilemmas will be much more complex. When dealing with business decisions, important questions to ask are:

- Who will be affected by this decision?
- What is the worst-case scenario for our clients, our colleagues, and the public?

- What are the alternatives to this decision?
- What are the downstream effects of this decision over the long term?

Summary

An ethical professional is one who is committed to doing the right thing every time, regardless of the situation. An ethical professional takes the rules of fair and responsible conduct seriously and takes all the necessary steps to abide by them. An ethical professional exercises independent judgment in determining the appropriate conduct in a given situation, creates relationships of trust, and demonstrates courageous behaviors when personal ethics are tested.

Bankers carry an extra burden of ethics, because bankers are trusted with other people's money. As a banker, you're entrusted with your customers' futures: their retirement, their children's education, their very quality of life. Any erosion in the public's trust of bankers can impact the stability of the U.S. financial markets. Bankers have increased ethical obligations because they often have fiduciary and agency relationships that require that they put clients' interests above their own. They must also act in good faith and with full disclosure.

Becoming an ethical banker requires a commitment to learning more about ethics through learning new behaviors and developing unique skills.

Ethics apply to your employee/employer relationship as well. Obligations to your employer run the gamut from showing up on time and putting in a full day's work to working at your full potential and speaking up when you witness unethical behavior. As an employee, you help fulfill the promises your employer makes to its customers.

The ethical organization has a clear vision, and integrity is valued throughout the organization. A highly ethical workplace is one where management embodies the vision, reward systems are aligned with the vision, and external and internal policies mirror the vision. Management leads through example and creates opportunities for employees to be involved in ethical decision making.

Every organization should create and communicate its code of ethics, including its internal policies and procedures. Membership in professional industry organizations with their own ethics policies and requirements often is another way to demonstrate comittment to ethical behavior.

While most organizations have their own codes of conduct, most include reference to three important foundations of professional ethics: honesty, innovation, and commitment.

But codes of conduct are only half of the equation; bankers must also embrace the opportunity to insist on ethical behavior in others. This means having the courage to report unethical behavior in an appropriate fashion. While our lives and those of our colleagues and loved ones are undeniably better when everyone plays by the rules, this is not always the case. Sometimes doing the right thing does not reap rewards in the short term. The only enduring reason to do the right thing is because it is the right thing to do.

CHAPTER 8

Managing Others: What Every Banker Needs to Know

After reading this chapter, you will be able to:

- Demonstrate understanding of general supervision concepts.
- Describe the important tools of supervision.
- Apply the Americans with Disabilities Act to hiring situations.
- Identify actions prohibited by various federal laws prohibiting discrimination.
- Describe the process of performance improvement.
- Describe effective teams.

Whether you are a supervisor or not, it's important to understand communication between subordinates and their bosses.

This chapter is directed primarily at the financial services manager or project leader with responsibility for supervising or managing the activities of other employees. A greater understanding of the supervisory process, however, will be useful in managing others and in performing your job to the satisfaction of your boss.

What Is Supervision?

The many types of supervisory roles can be grouped into three categories:

1. Task supervision
2. Project supervision
3. Administrative supervision

A task supervisor oversees employees performing a particular function. A project supervisor coordinates the efforts of employees from various areas toward a specific project goal. An administrative supervisor supports an employee with approvals and authority related to policies and procedures. Since all types of supervisors work closely with people, they need to have excellent leadership skills.

Task Supervision

Task supervision is used for operational functions—those that are performed regularly by a group of people in established jobs with somewhat stable responsibilities. Task supervision is the most direct and historically common form of supervision. When you are a task supervisor, you:

- Assign work.
- Review work.
- Train.
- Evaluate performance.

Say you are a task supervisor of a workgroup of customer service representatives who answer phone calls to resolve customer account problems. In this case, you

- Schedule the work shifts.
- Oversee the call volume and distribution.
- Field inquiries that require supervisor attention.
- Listen in on calls to check the quality of the representatives' work, as necessary.

To perform task supervision effectively, a supervisor generally needs to be able to do the task. Thus, you would make a poor customer service supervisor if you did not know how to handle customer calls yourself. An excellent teller, however, is a good candidate for head teller. Someone who already performs a job function well is often promoted to supervise others doing the same job. A task supervisor must possess excellent organizational and training skills.

In financial services organizations, task supervision generally follows the organizational chart, meaning higher-ups supervise the tasks of their subordinates. Many times the task supervisor also performs the tasks at hand. The loan department manager, for example, supervises the work tasks of the loan specialists. That manager might also see loan customers on a regular basis.

Project Supervision

As opposed to task supervision, which focuses on operational work and closely follows the organizational chart, project supervision focuses on developmental work to achieve a specific goal using a team of people across functional areas.

Say you are asked to lead a project team charged with improving customer service throughout your insurance organization. The members on your team are

- Accounts payable manager
- Customer service representative
- Systems analyst
- Personal banker

The employees on the team may not report to you on the organizational chart. Rather, the team is brought together to improve customer service and is disbanded when the project is complete.

Project supervisors, also called project managers, generally are not able to do the work of all project team members. In fact, team members often are selected based on individual expertise, so a project manager might not be able to do the tasks of any particular team member. In contrast to task supervision, which is ongoing, project supervision is oriented toward a particular goal. A project supervisor must have superior planning and delegation ability.

As more organizations streamline their operations, eliminate layers of middle management, and prepare to respond to rapidly changing customer needs, more task supervisors are being asked to take on project supervision responsibilities. In general, the project team structure is considered a faster and more flexible way to get work done. As a supervisor in the financial services industry, you may be asked to fill both roles: task supervision and project supervision.

Administrative Supervision

Every employee in an organization requires some administrative support, such as:

- Authorizing vacation time
- Signing for tuition reimbursement
- Consulting scheduling or benefits

Many supervisors, whether task supervisors or project supervisors, also serve in this administrative role. If you sign time cards and authorizations for employee benefits in your workgroup, you probably are also the administrative supervisor of that group. An administrative supervisor must know how to motivate and support employees.

Communication

You may think that communication is a simple process: Just tell someone what you want and that person will understand you. Transmitting information to another person is a sophisticated process, however, and it requires your attention each step of the way. In this chapter, we'll discuss interpersonal communication based on the model in Exhibit 8.1.

In this model, the sender first encodes an idea into language. The language then travels over a transmission channel—the phone, perhaps, or e-mail, or in-person conversation. At the other side of the transmission, the receiver decodes the idea and delivers feedback to the sender.

The process of *encoding* and *decoding* involves selecting words to represent thoughts. Because each of us uses language differently and has different language skills, the encoding and decoding steps of the communication process are likely problem areas.

You make this statement to an employee: "I expect you to settle all simple claims quickly." In this statement, the word *quickly* might mean within 3 business days to you, but the employee might decode the word *quickly* as 2 weeks or 10 business days.

EXHIBIT 8.1

Four-Stage Communication Process Model

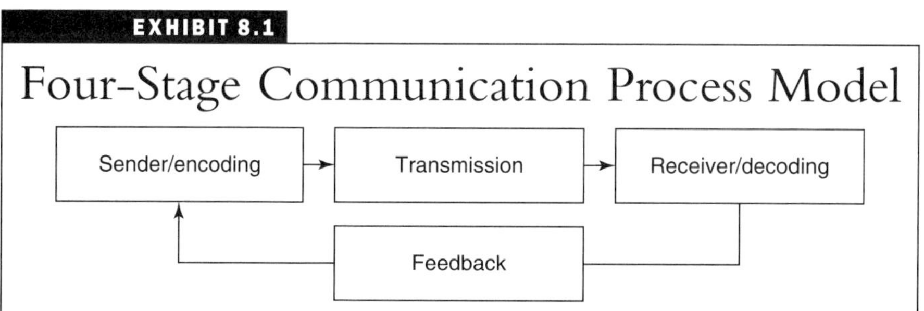

Encoding and decoding can get even more complicated when the sender and receiver have different first languages or widely different cultural backgrounds.

Transmission can be complicated as well, depending upon the complexity of the communication. Selecting an appropriate transmission channel is critical to good communication. Possible channels are:

- In-person
- E-mail
- Telephone

In the Real World

Problem

It is noon and you need to remind a new worker to send end-of-the-day reports. You know that e-mail is checked in the morning. What is the best channel to use to transmit this message?

- In-person
- E-mail
- Telephone

Answer

E-mail would not be a good transmission channel for sending an urgent message about end-of-day reports. A telephone call or an in-person conversation would be more appropriate, so you could be sure that the employee receives and understands the message.

Problem

You need to send your employees a budget forecast with numerical and statistical information. Which channel would be best to transmit the information?

In the Real World (continued)

- In-person
- E-mail
- Telephone

Answer

It would be better to transmit the information through e-mail, so your employees can refer to details later.

Once a message has been transmitted, the response to a message is called *feedback.* Feedback can be as simple as an employee nodding her head during an in-person conversation or as formal as an employee submitting a written response to a performance evaluation. Feedback might not contain agreement or disagreement; it might simply convey the fact that your message was received.

In general, lack of feedback is a problem between employees and supervisors. Employees may acknowledge receipt of the message but are reluctant to tell supervisors that they disagree with its contents or cannot meet its expectations. So, as a supervisor, it is your responsibility to structure the feedback process. You can do this by requesting feedback:

> In a staff meeting, you could ask: "What do you think of this schedule, John?"
>
> In a written memo, you could state: "Please have your comments to me by June 11."

Due to the nature of the relationship, supervisors hold more responsibility for the communication process than do their employees. Supervisors must understand the four-step communication process and seek to make improvements at each step. Ask yourself these five questions:

1. Do I encode messages clearly, using details and objective terms to describe my expectations?
2. Am I choosing the appropriate transmission channel for different types of messages?
3. Are my employees decoding my messages in the way I intend?
4. Are my employees providing feedback to me, so that I know they understand my messages?
5. Am I open to all types of feedback, not just agreement?

Delegation and Reporting

Appropriate delegation of authority is a balance between absentee supervision and micromanagement. It's important for a supervisor to find and maintain this equilibrium. An effective status-reporting process can help you stay abreast of your employees' progress, plans, and concerns. Status meetings are the place to create team attitude and vision in your workgroup. Supervisors who regularly recognize their employees' contributions in a variety of ways are rewarded with superior workgroup achievements.

At some time in our work lives, most of us have had an absent supervisor. That's the manager who couldn't be found when an irate customer wanted to know why his loan was turned down. It's the one who always ducked into her office as soon as the perennial conflict between two difficult co-workers gained momentum.

At some time in our careers, most of us also have had a micromanager. That's the supervisor who was at each person's desk tapping his foot at exactly the moment lunch hour ended. The one who made changes in memos and reports just to impart his own editorial style.

The balance between being an absent supervisor and being a micromanager is hard to strike, but it's very important to try. If you follow these five tips, it will be impossible for you to avoid your employees' workday problems or to manage their work down to the minutest details.

1. Practice compassion and empathy.
2. Avoid being overly critical.
3. Make yourself available.
4. Show interest in employees.
5. Remain open to ideas.

Status Reporting

One tool that supervisors use to understand their employees' progress and concerns is the status report. There are many ways to write status reports, but most contain these sections:

- Completed work
- Upcoming work
- Problems
- Comments

The completed work section is where your employees can tell you which tasks they've accomplished. In an operational setting, such as the estate planning department, an employee might report on how many customers she assisted and how many were referred to the trust and legal departments.

In the upcoming work section, employees outline what they intend to accomplish in the next time period. Knowing an employee's upcoming plans can help you staff the department so that any call-in or walk-in customers can receive help immediately. For example, an estate planning specialist's upcoming work might include:

- A training seminar on new Roth IRA regulations on Monday and Tuesday
- Sales calls for the rest of the week

The problems section is where employees can inform you of support they need from you to do their jobs effectively. Of course, employees will have to perceive that you are open to this feedback before they will feel comfortable including it in their reports. As an example, the estate planning specialist might let you know that many customer calls are rolling over into voice mail at peak lunchtime hours, when working people generally call to complete their estate planning business with the bank. She might remind you that you have set an expectation for the department that no customer receives a voice mail message during regular business hours.

In the comments section, employees can list any other information they think you might need to supervise the group effectively. The estate planning specialist, for example, might point out the excellent service provided by the investment group or mention that she noticed a few referrals from an outside attorney whose name she hasn't seen on the referral list before.

Acting on this type of information is what sets an excellent supervisor, and workgroup, apart from a simply adequate one. If you can cultivate a supervisory environment in which your employees feel free to report problems and make comments to you, you will benefit greatly from the effort.

Staff Meetings

In addition to regular status reporting, most supervisors convene some type of staff meeting on a regular basis. The purpose of meetings is to:

- Create a joint vision.
- Clarify departmental or project goals.
- Delegate tasks.
- Plan jointly.
- Generate ideas.
- Understand the issues your employees face.

If you wish to foster a team attitude in your staff meetings, leave the details to the status reports. In addition, make sure that staff meetings are not the only time your employees see you. Most successful supervisors use some version of the management-by-walking-around technique.

Employee Recognition

Have you ever had a supervisor take credit for an idea or work product that was yours? Do you remember how you felt? Do you ever want an employee of yours to feel that way?

If you want your employees to reach their goals regularly, you'll need to find ways to recognize their efforts. All of us perform better when we know that our work is valued and appreciated. There are many informal ways to privately and publicly acknowledge an employee's efforts between performance reviews.

No matter which type of supervisor you are, you will be responsible for creating clear, specific, measurable performance objectives for your employees and for assessing their performance periodically during the year, not only at performance review time. Successful supervisors find creative ways to deliver positive consequences to high performers in addition to the financial rewards offered by the performance management process.

Your bank probably has an established performance management process. Each year at a specific time, supervisors evaluate the work of their employees, give an overall rating, and distribute pay raises based on performance levels. Perhaps this process seems like busywork to you, or maybe it appears to be arbitrary and not worth the effort. However, effectively implemented, the performance management process is an excellent tool for effective supervision.

A formal, strategic performance management system:

- Uses financial, strategic, and operating business measures to gauge how well a company meets its targets
- Translates these company performance measures into business unit strategy plans and individual incentive compensation

Even if your organization has not yet developed a strategic performance management system, you can still incorporate organizational goals into your employees' performance objectives.

Whatever the performance management process used, it is crucial that you set specific, measurable objectives. Statements may represent valid goals; however, they may be too vague to be objectives because they are hard to quantify.

TIPS AND TECHNIQUES

Goals: Not Measurable as Stated	Objectives: Specific, Measurable
Minimize customer wait times in the lobby.	Monitor customer line in the lobby. When five or more people are waiting, notify a standby teller. If the line again reaches five or more people, notify the supervisor.
Provide timely problem resolution.	Return all customer phone calls or e-mails the same day they are received. If a problem cannot be resolved at the time of the call, provide the customer with a specific day and time by which the problem will be resolved. Mark all follow-up days and times on the departmental problem calendar.
Increase skills in network administration.	Attend a Certified Network Administrator class and pass the certification test within three months of class.

If you use the specific, measurable performance objectives to evaluate employee performance on a regular basis, the annual performance appraisal will be much easier. But don't wait until the annual appraisal to use the information. As you gather data, give periodic feedback that updates the employee on whether his or her performance is meeting objectives—while there is still a chance to correct the situation.

Your task as a supervisor conducting performance evaluations is to deliver appropriate consequences. Your performance management process probably provides you with some alternatives. There may be a rating scale for each performance objective:

- Needs improvement
- Meets expectations
- Exceeds expectations

Your organization's process may also tie pay increases to an employee's overall performance rating.

Project Management Skills

The role of project supervisor requires special skills because of the diversity of the team being managed. While task supervisors gain their authority through the organizational hierarchy, project leaders must demonstrate their ability to assume authority in a project team. When you begin to lead a project, you should place the project goal within the context of your organization's mission and strategic plan and then choose an approach to project planning that suits your purposes. Whichever project planning methodology you use, keep in mind that assessing progress is the single most important task a project supervisor performs.

As discussed earlier in this chapter, the leadership role of task supervisors is supported by the formal structure of the organizational chart. In contrast, however, project managers often coordinate the work of interdisciplinary teams of people, some of whom might be their organizational peers or perhaps even hold positions higher on the organizational chart.

If you are asked to supervise the work of a project team, you will need to rely on your own skills to create the credibility and authority you bring to the role.

Once you've established your authority, the real work begins. You are given a charge or goal from a manager or executive. Before you begin the project, find out how your project goal fits within the overall direction of your organization. To do this, you might have to locate a few important documents.

First find your organization's mission statement. It is a short summary of the purpose of the organization's activities. Next review the strategic plan, a document that sets the direction for your organization's activities for the next several years. If your organization doesn't have a mission statement or a strategic plan, ask your own manager to explain the overall direction of the organization and how your project fits into these plans.

Clarifying Project Goals

The mission and strategic plan gives a context for your project. Next you can begin to clarify what your project team is expected to accomplish.

When you have clarified and established the scope and specific goal of the project, you should communicate it clearly to your team members. You might even invite a manager or executive to your project team's kickoff meeting to state in person what the goals of the project are and to field any questions.

Planning

There are many approaches to project planning in the business world. Perhaps your organization already uses a set of structured project planning techniques, called a *methodology*. Regardless of the methodology you use, you should become familiar with these terms:

Deliverable An object or product that results from the work of the project group; this could be a document, a computer program, a training session, a process, a policy, and so on.

Goal The objective marking the end point of the project.

Milestone Intermediate objectives in the project—for instance, creating a short list of 3 call center automation programs from the 10 originally reviewed.

Phase A segment of project activities. Many times project phases carry names such as Needs Assessment, Implementation, and Quality Assurance.

Assessing Progress

Assessing the progress of the project is one of the most important duties of a project supervisor. Keeping a project on track requires an organized and diligent supervisor.

Each employee on your project team should have a clear set of tasks and due dates for all project activities, and that includes you as the supervisor. You should establish a regular time—weekly, for instance—to review each team member's progress, remind team members of tasks due, and adjust dates if necessary.

To be an effective supervisor, you will need to continually assess your own skills and performance and find ways to improve them. Joining professional organizations and gathering information through publications and web sites can be a very effective way to improve your supervisory knowledge.

While success in reaching your career goals begins with a frank assessment of your own skills, knowledge, and performance, it ultimately depends on your willingness to take the steps necessary to improve yourself. Where should you start?

You can begin by taking stock of your own performance. Here are some examples of questions you may wish to consider:

- Is your supervisory role task, project, or administration oriented? Are you clear on what your employees expect from you?
- How do your communication skills measure up? Do you attend to each step of the communication cycle? How are your writing skills?
- Are you familiar with the mission and strategic plan of your organization? Do you integrate your workgroup's goals, and the

performance objectives of each employee, with those overarching directives?

- Where do you stand on the absentee-versus-micromanaging supervisor continuum?
- Do you set specific and measurable performance criteria for your employees? Do you give them performance feedback frequently throughout the year?

If you answered "no" to any of these questions, you've found a good place to start your self-development efforts.

Advanced Supervision

Now that we've covered the basics, we can explore a group of advanced supervision concepts with examples drawn from banking, accounting, and investment environments.

- *Interviewing skills* are critical for screening, selecting, hiring, and retaining the most qualified applicants.

Most companies recognize the crucial importance of hiring the right people for the right jobs:

- Employee *productivity* is key to company performance.
- Employee *turnover* is very expensive.

Each step in the hiring process—recruiting, screening, hiring, orienting, and training—is associated with both direct and indirect costs.

Selecting the best candidate for the job is one of the most cost-effective supervisory efforts you can undertake. Your interviewing techniques can make the difference between hiring highly effective long-term employees and experiencing costly turnover in critical positions. Exhibits 8.2 and 8.3 show and compare structured and unstructured interview formats.

EXHIBIT 8.2

Structured versus Unstructured Interview Formats

Structured Format

Identical questions are asked of each candidate.

Unstructured Format

Questions and direction of the interview are tailored to the individual being interviewed, in a more free-form approach.

Structured Interview Questions

1. Introduce the panel
2. Why do you want this position?
3. Which of your skills will be most important to this position?
4. Do you have any questions about the position?

Unstructured Interview

- Introduction
- Job description
- Background
- Questions?

EXHIBIT 8.3

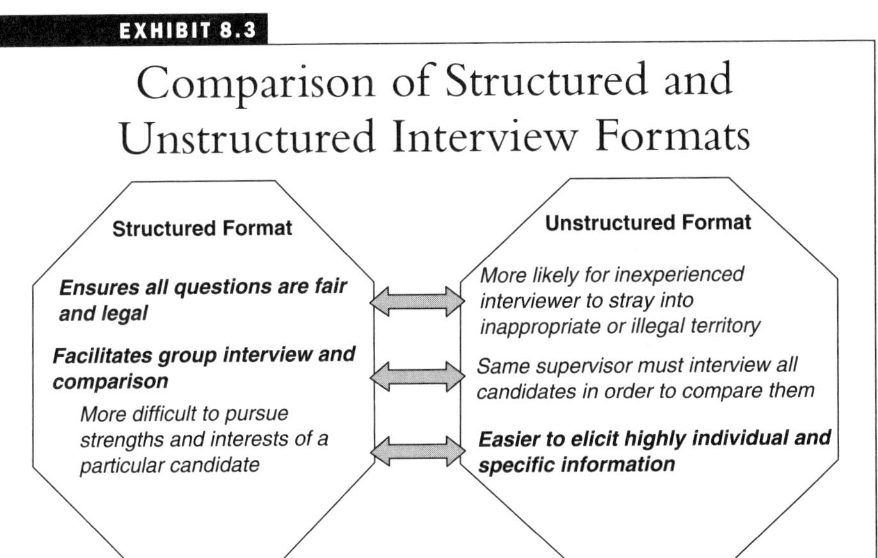

Applying the Americans with Disabilities Act

Federal and state laws govern whether and how employers can question an employment candidate about:

- Physical disability
- Mental disability
- Emotional disability

Various federal and state courts have ruled that these conditions are all considered disabilities:

- Obesity
- Suicide attempts
- Posttraumatic stress disorder
- Alcoholism

In all cases, it's best to confine yourself to asking only for information directly related to the candidate's ability to perform specific tasks required by the job. Even casual interview questions that delve into a candidate's personal life are inappropriate.

- The stipulations of the Americans with Disabilities Act (ADA) apply to the vast majority of employers, public and private, in the country.

Employment discrimination is prohibited against "qualified individuals with disabilities." This includes applicants as well as employees. Employment discrimination under ADA is also prohibited against persons who have a known association or relationship with an individual with a disability.

TIPS AND TECHNIQUES

Disability Defined

According to the ADA, an individual is considered to have a *disability* if:

- She or he has a physical or mental impairment that substantially limits one or more major life activities, or
- Has a record of such impairment, or
- Is regarded as having such impairment

The first part of the definition makes clear that the ADA applies to persons who have impairments and that these must substantially limit major life activities. Table 8.1 provides examples of covered and noncovered impairments.

The second part of the definition protects individuals with a record of a disability, such as those who have recovered from cancer or mental illness.

The third part of the definition protects individuals who are regarded as having a substantially limiting impairment, even though they may not have such impairment. For example, this provision would protect a qualified individual with a severe facial disfigurement from being denied employment because an employer feared the "negative reactions" of customers or co-workers.

A qualified individual with a disability is a person who:

- Meets legitimate skill, experience, education, or other requirements of an employment position that she or he holds or seeks

TABLE 8.1

Coverage of Current Impairments

Examples of Covered Limited Activities	Examples of Covered Illnesses	Examples of Conditions Generally Not Covered
Seeing Hearing Speaking Walking Breathing Performing manual tasks Learning Caring for oneself Working	Epilepsy Paralysis HIV infection AIDS Substantial hearing or visual impairment Mental retardation Specific learning disability	Minor, nonchronic conditions of short duration, such as: sprain, broken limb, flu

- Can perform the essential functions of the position with or without reasonable accommodation

To determine whether a person meets the definition of a "qualified individual with a disability," you need to:

- Differentiate between the essential functions of the job and the marginal or incidental job functions.
- Consider whether a disabled individual who is qualified to perform essential job functions except for limitations caused by a disability could perform essential functions with a reasonable accommodation.

If a written job description has been prepared in advance of advertising or interviewing applicants for a job, this will be considered as evidence, although not conclusive evidence, of the essential functions of the job.

No hiring preference among qualified applicants must be given. An employer is free to select the most qualified applicant available and to make decisions based on reasons unrelated to a disability.

Example

Job: Typist
Requirements: Type 75 words per minute accurately

Applicant #1:

- An individual with a disability
- Is provided with a reasonable accommodation for a typing test
- Accurately types 50 words per minute

Applicant #2:

- Has no disability
- Accurately types 75 words per minute

Hiring decision: The employer can hire the applicant with the higher typing speed, if typing speed is needed for successful performance of the job.

Medical Examinations and Inquiries about Disability

The following chart illustrates some of the restrictions on questions that can be asked of applicants with regard to potential disabilities. It also describes accepted questions about the applicant's ability to do the job.

Prior to Job Offer	As a Condition of Job Offer
An employer may not ask or require a job applicant to: • Take a medical examination before making a job offer. • Make any pre-employment disclosure about a disability or the nature or severity of a disability. An employer may: • Ask questions about the ability to perform specific job functions. • With certain limitations, ask an individual with a disability to describe or demonstrate how he or she would perform these functions.	An employer may condition a job offer on the satisfactory result of a postoffer medical examination or medical inquiry if this is required of all entering employees in the same job category. A postoffer examination or inquiry does not have to be job-related or consistent with business necessity. However, acceptable reasons for failure to hire because of results of a postoffer exam must be job-related or consistent with business necessity.

A failure to hire because of a direct threat (the term *direct threat* means a significant risk to the health or safety of others that cannot be eliminated by reasonable accommodation) is considered job-related and consistent with business necessity if:

- A postoffer medical examination or inquiry reveals a disability that the employer can demonstrate would pose a direct threat in the workplace.
- The direct threat cannot be eliminated or reduced below the direct threat level through reasonable accommodation, *and*
- The employer can show that no reasonable accommodation was available that would enable the individual to perform the essential job functions, *or*
- The employer can show that accommodation would impose an undue hardship.

A postoffer medical examination may not disqualify an individual with a disability who is currently able to perform essential job functions because of speculation that the disability may cause a risk of future injury.

After a person starts work, a medical examination or inquiry of an employee must be job-related and consistent with business necessity. Employers may conduct employee medical examinations:

- Where there is evidence of a job performance or safety problem
- As required by other federal laws
- To determine current fitness to perform a particular job
- On a voluntary basis as part of an employee health program

Tests for illegal use of drugs are not medical examinations under the ADA and are not subject to the restrictions of such examinations.

Information from all medical examinations and inquiries must be kept apart from general personnel files as a separate, confidential medical record, available only under limited conditions.

Pre-employment Inquiries

A pre-employment inquiry about a disability is allowed if required by another federal law or regulation, such as those applicable to disabled veterans and veterans of the Vietnam era. Pre-employment inquiries about disabilities may be necessary to identify applicants or clients with disabilities in order to provide them with required special services.

Individuals with disabilities may be invited to identify themselves on a job application form or by other pre-employment inquiry, to satisfy affirmative action or other federal requirements.

Meeting Equal Employment Opportunity Commission (EEOC) Guidelines

The Equal Employment Opportunity Commission (EEOC) enforces the employment provisions of the ADA laws. The EEOC also provides oversight and coordination of all federal equal employment opportunity regulations, practices, and policies.

IN THE REAL WORLD

Equal Pay Act of 1963 (EPA)	Protects men and women who perform substantially equal work in the same establishment from sex-based wage discrimination
Age Discrimination in Employment Act of 1967 (ADEA)	Protects individuals who are 40 years of age or older
Section 501 of the Rehabilitation Act of 1973	Prohibits discrimination against qualified individuals with disabilities who work in the federal government
Civil Rights Act of 1991	Provides monetary damages in cases of intentional employment discrimination

It is against federal law to discriminate against job candidates based on personal characteristics that are unrelated to their ability to perform the job at hand. Besides the legality of the situation, it simply doesn't make business sense to overlook potentially productive members of your team simply due to race, sex, or any other equally irrelevant factors. Wise supervisors know that building a competent, performance-oriented workgroup enhances their own reputations.

Under Title VII, the ADA, and the ADEA, it is illegal to discriminate in any aspect of employment, including:

- Hiring and firing
- Compensation, assignment, or classification of employees
- Transfer, promotion, layoff, or recall
- Job advertisements
- Recruitment
- Testing
- Use of company facilities
- Training and apprenticeship programs
- Fringe benefits
- Pay, retirement plans, and disability leave
- Other terms and conditions of employment
- Harassment on the basis of race, color, religion, sex, national origin, disability, or age
- Retaliation against an individual for filing a charge of discrimination, participating in an investigation, or opposing discriminatory practices
- Employment decisions based on stereotypes or assumptions about the abilities, traits, or performance of individuals of a certain sex, race, age, religion, or ethnic group, or individuals with disabilities
- Denying employment opportunities to a person because of marriage to, or association with, an individual of a particular race, religion, national origin, or an individual with a disability
- Discrimination because of participation in schools or places of worship associated with a particular racial, ethnic, or religious group.

Employers are required to post notices to all employees advising them of their rights under the laws EEOC enforces and their right to be free from retaliation. Such notices must be accessible, as needed, to persons with visual or other disabilities that affect reading.

Assuring Confidentiality

The courts have clarified how, when, and to whom employers can release information about employees or people who interview for employment.

Your financial services organization probably has a policy for giving employment references. Many companies restrict managers to giving:

- Dates of employment
- Job title

Whatever your organizational policy is, you should be aware of it and follow it to the letter.

Follow these confidentiality guidelines when discussing employee performance and issues such as attendance, pay rate, and personal information:

- Share information only on a need-to-know basis. Under no circumstances should you divulge personal or employment information about one employee to another, or anyone else, unless that other person needs to know this information to perform a job-related task.

  When possible, information should be communicated by the employee, not by you.
- Any personal information an employee shares with you should stay between you two.

  If an employee confides in you about difficulties with a domestic partner, you should assume the information is private and not to be shared in the workgroup.

  If an employee informs you of the need for sick leave to have reconstructive plastic surgery for a scar from an automobile accident, you should tell co-workers only that the worker will be away from work for a particular period.

Remember, trust is an important element of any highly productive workgroup. If you wish to keep the channels of communication open between you and your employees, you must first demonstrate to them that you can be trusted with sensitive and confidential information. As a supervisor, your trustworthiness is a crucial element of your professional reputation. *Guard it closely!*

As discussed earlier in this chapter, the communication process consists of four steps:

1. Sender encoding
2. Transmission
3. Receiver decoding
4. Feedback

There are several possible pitfalls in this process:

- Encoding and decoding fail when the sender and receiver use language differently.
- Transmission fails when the sender chooses the wrong channel.
- Feedback fails when the feedback channel is not perceived as open and effective.

Because supervisors control many of the opportunities for communication, they bear the responsibility for ensuring that communication among workgroup members and between supervisor and employees goes smoothly.

Successful supervisors always look for gaps in communication before criticizing an employee's performance. Improving communication skills is a wise approach to creating a high-performing team.

Conflict Management

There are a variety of tests for supervisors to measure employees:

- Personality

- Decision making
- Learning style
- Communication style

The information you gain from these tests can shed light on both big and small problems occurring in your workgroup.

Efforts to resolve conflict should address these possible causes—differences in personality, decision making, learning style, and communication style—first and then proceed to negotiation if a conflict still exists. Managers who instill a sense of individual responsibility for conflict resolution among their employees will have a more self-sufficient workgroup.

Despite all efforts to understand each employee's personality, learning style, and communication weaknesses, conflict will inevitably erupt in any workplace. The first thing to do is to introduce a cooling-off period. Once everyone is calm, you can introduce a structured environment in which the parties can begin to work out their differences. Often resolution of the conflict requires negotiation. As many business experts agree, negotiation is a skill worth developing.

While it might be tempting to intervene in all interpersonal conflicts in your workgroup, it is important that you help your employees develop strong communication and negotiation skills for themselves. Some of the best executives maintain that they know they're doing a good job if they can walk away from their organizations for a period of time and no changes occur in the way the organization is run.

Employee Development

There are many tools and tests available for assessing employee knowledge and skills. Job training is related to an employee's current position, while career advancement training prepares an employee to take a promotion or another job. Providing tuition reimbursement for employees to pursue college degrees can be a powerful retention strategy.

Supervisors should always try to identify and develop employees with supervisory potential.

Providing Job Training

Job training increases employee skills for their current position. It takes many forms:

- Seminars and workshops
- College courses
- Online courses
- One-on-one training with a peer or supervisor

Think of the benefits to your organization when they are asked to provide career advancement training—it leads to retaining good employees for the organization, although often in a different position. It is less expensive in the long run than losing the employee altogether.

Check your own company's job descriptions. Odds are nearly all salaried positions require at least a bachelor's degree. To advance from nonexempt positions to professional ones, your employees have to pursue a degree.

Fortunately, universities are making more room for nontraditional, adult, working students. In addition, more and more companies are offering tuition reimbursement as a way to retain employees.

If your human resources department has a tuition reimbursement program in place, familiarize yourself with it so you can answer your employees' questions regarding which courses and degree programs are approved for reimbursement.

While a bachelor's degree provides a very important background in critical thinking, writing, logic, and analytical skills, it doesn't necessarily have to be in finance or accounting to improve a financial services worker's job skills.

Planning for Succession

One of your career goals probably includes promotion to another position, either with your organization or another one. Who will step up to take your place as supervisor? Have you identified several team members and begun to groom them to succeed you? If not, you should. Succession planning, which is the process of preparing employees to step into your own role, is an important supervisory responsibility. A successful succession planning process identifies the leadership styles and skills of each potential succession candidate as well as the gaps and potential of the candidates and creates an advancement plan for each one.

If you have the budget resources, you could hire a management consultant to help you reach these succession planning objectives, or you can do a good deal of succession planning on your own by following these steps:

- Discover your employees' career goals.
- Identify employees who are the best candidates for future supervisory positions.
- Include career advancement training for employees identified in your succession plans.

Performance Improvement

A supervisor is responsible for establishing performance objectives that guide employees and provide a means to assess performance. Clear and measurable performance objectives are the basis of any solid performance appraisal process, including identifying unsatisfactory performance.

One common time to identify performance problems is during the annual performance appraisal. In many cases, notice of poor performance and implementation of an appropriate performance improvement plan solves the problem. However, in some cases, more will be required to identify the causes of the poor performance and to help the employee discover ways to improve.

Poor performance can be caused by work-related or personal circumstances:

Cause of Poor Performance	Remedy
Work-related issues	Provide appropriate training and interventions.
Personality conflicts	
Variances in learning styles	
Gaps in communication skills	
Lack of job skills	
Personal issues	Help employees understand the effect the circumstance is having on performance.
Family problems	Inform employees of available resources, such as an Employee Assistance Program that provides sensitive and confidential services to help with difficult personal situations, including referrals to outside services.
Mental illness	
Substance abuse	

Here are some techniques you can use to enhance performance:

- *Mentoring.* Match the employee with a peer or supervisor who has strong skills in the employee's weak area. The employee gains knowledge by discussing the proper performance and observing the mentor performing related tasks.
- *Results contract.* Have the employee establish goals for performance improvement and dates for reaching them. Establish clear consequences if the goals are not met.

- *Daily meetings.* Arrange to meet with the poorly performing employee daily to prioritize tasks (if production is the problem) or discuss how to perform tasks (if skills are the issue).
- *360-degree feedback.* Have all workgroup employees give performance feedback to one another, so those poor performers can understand how their work impacts others.

When you develop a performance improvement plan with the employee, create a schedule for revisiting the plan and assessing progress. Provide consistent and clear feedback on how the employee is progressing.

Unfortunately, there will be some employees whose performance will not improve no matter what techniques you try. As a supervisor, it is your responsibility to recognize unwilling and resistant poor performers and to minimize their impact on the workgroup and organization by proceeding with disciplinary action and even dismissal if necessary.

Managing for Excellence

A workgroup achieves excellence by working as a team, in an environment of collaboration, to reach common goals. In addition to addressing poor performance, supervisors must reward top performers in their workgroups to maintain the team's effectiveness. A focus on continuous improvement ensures that workgroups contribute to the success of the organization.

As a supervisor, you must support both the individuals working on the team and the common goals toward which the team is working. Here are some examples of the types of teams that exist in organizations:

- Cross-functional teams
- Teams with common customers or business areas
- Teams with remote or telecommuting members

For all types of teams, a focus on performance leads to the most success. Thus, as a supervisor, you must establish well-defined expectations if you expect your team to reach its goals.

Collaboration, as opposed to competition, is an important element of teamwork. We've all encountered co-workers who hoard information or resources in order to save glory for themselves and deny it to others.

A supervisor can encourage collaboration in these ways:

- Make the team's success a factor in each member's appraisal.
- Create ways for employees to learn from and be rewarded for teaching each other.
- Weave team goals into each employee's performance objectives.
- Model and point out examples of cooperative behavior.

Rather than creating an inscribed award for employee of the month or giving away a gift certificate, think of job-related ways to reward employees for outstanding work. Help your employees understand that excellent performance is in their best career interests.

As the pace of change accelerates in financial services, supervisors will face more and more frequent challenges to modify services in response to customer concerns. To be among those leaders, you will need to position yourself always to be on the leading edge of positive change in your organization.

To be an effective supervisor, continually assess your own skills and performance and find ways to improve. As a supervisor, you may be targeting a management- or executive-level position as your next career move. In general, these categories of skills are needed at the management level. Work on areas where your skills and experience are lacking:

- Budget development, maintenance, and reporting
- Operations and computer systems
- Staff hiring, supervision, and performance management
- Interdisciplinary or cross-functional teams and committees

Summary

In this chapter we learned that supervision can be grouped into three categories: task supervision, project supervision, and administrative supervision.

A task supervisor oversees employees performing a particular function. A project supervisor coordinates the efforts of employees from various areas toward a specific project goal. An administrative supervisor supports an employee with approvals and authority related to policies and procedures. Leadership skills are important at all levels of the organization and for all types of supervisors.

Communication is an integral part of the leadership process and a key leadership skill for supervisors. Another skill is appropriate delegation of authority. Finding the balance between absentee supervision and micromanagement is an important skill to have, but it is not always easy to develop. A good supervisor must find the balance—the middle ground. Once work is delegated, supervisors must create clear, specific, and measurable performance objectives for employees and assess their performance against those objectives.

When you supervise the work of a project team, you'll need to rely on your own skills to create credibility and authority. This is because often project managers coordinate interdisciplinary project teams of people, some of whom are organizational peers or even hold positions higher on the organizational chart.

Screening, selecting, hiring, and retaining the most qualified applicants take excellent interviewing skills. Hiring the right people is critical because productivity is key to company performance. Not only that, employee turnover is very expensive. Interviewing techniques and formats can be a critical differentiator in attracting the right talent.

Federal and state laws govern whether and how employers can question candidates about physical, mental, and emotional disabilities. In hiring, employers may not discriminate against candidates with disabilities. The Equal Employment Opportunity Commission enforces the laws and provides oversight and coordination of all federal equal employment opportunity regulations.

Interpersonal conflict can arise among employees from differences in communication styles, personality types, and learning styles. It is the supervisor's responsibility to understand each employee's personality, learning style, and communication weaknesses and to facilitate conflict resolution. Often resolution of conflict requires negotiation, a skill that is useful for supervisors to develop.

In addition to their own development, good supervisors encourage employee development through internal training, tuition reimbursement, and other programs. Succession planning, the process of preparing employees to step into your own role, is an important supervisory responsibility.

CHAPTER 9

The Market: It's Bigger than You Think

After reading this chapter, you will be able to:

- Understand the four steps to develop a marketing plan.
- Describe how to increase market share and share of customer.
- Explain how to manage the life cycle of your product or service.
- Communicate how to identify competitors, and analyze your own performance.

Banking today is more complex than ever. Even the best-run banks need to constantly reexamine their approach to growing their business. Marketing is a critical component to these efforts. Good marketing brings to together the products and services of the bank with the customer who wishes to buy the product or service.

Introduction to Marketing

The marketing process links the efforts of businesses to produce and sell products that meet the desires of their customers. The role of marketing is to ensure that a business has and uses market knowledge and expertise.

- Sales is not a substitute for the marketing process. When businesses leapfrog to sales, they end up struggling to sell products that competitors already offer or customers do not want. And as a result, they do not have the benefit of a carefully researched market position.

According to the American Marketing Association, "marketing is the process of planning and executing the conception, pricing, promotion and distribution of ideas, goods and services to create exchanges that satisfy individual and corporate goals."

If marketing is successful, there is a transfer of a product from the seller to the buyer. Marketing is the link between a business and its customers. Through the marketing process, successful businesses:

- Ask "What does our customer want to buy?"
- Tailor all elements of the marketing process to meet those desires.

Ultimately, marketing creates a win-win partnership between the buyer and the seller of goods and services (see Exhibit 9.1).

Since marketing is the link between a business and its customer, you can bet that it plays an important role in business success. A good marketing program ensures that a business:

- Has a clear understanding of its business environment, competition, customers, market trends, and applicable rules and regulations
- Uses its market knowledge and expertise to develop and sustain mutually beneficial relationships with its customers

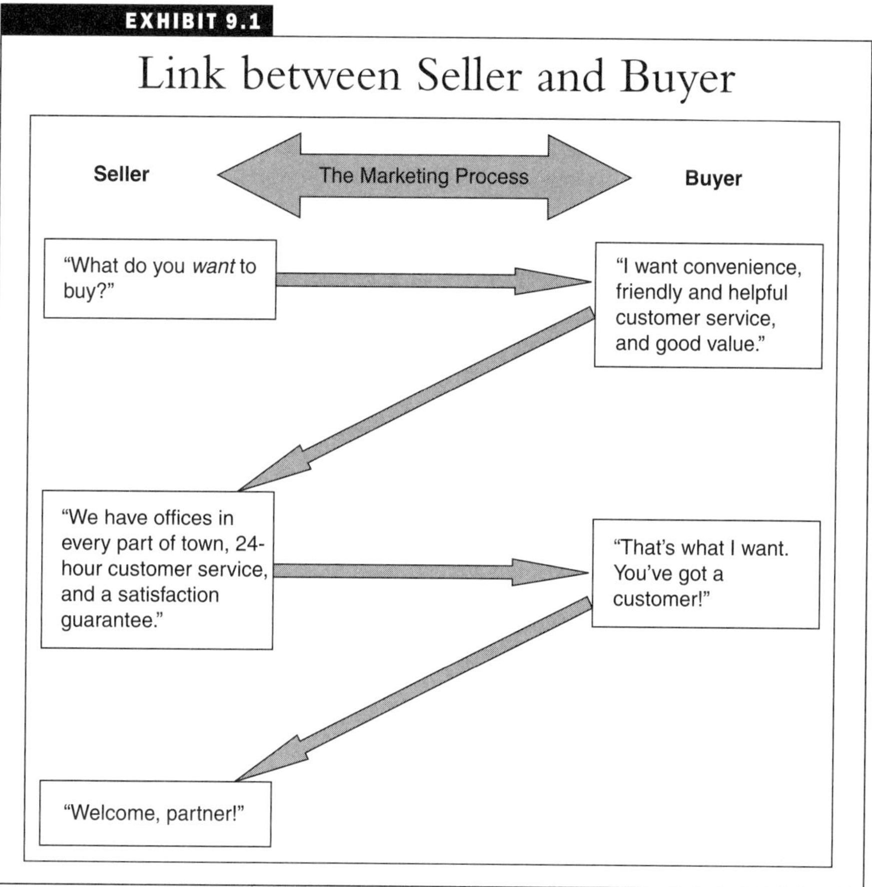

If your marketing is strong, you know what you're selling, who you're up against, and what threats or opportunities are on the business horizon.

If you're a good marketer, you:

- Know what your ideal customer wants and needs.
- Tailor your products, services, and messages to build a win-win buyer–seller relationship.

The road from customer knowledge to customer satisfaction involves many stops along the way. As Exhibit 9.2 illustrates, the marketing process involves research, product development, pricing, packaging, distribution, advertising and promotion, sales, and customer service.

EXHIBIT 9.2

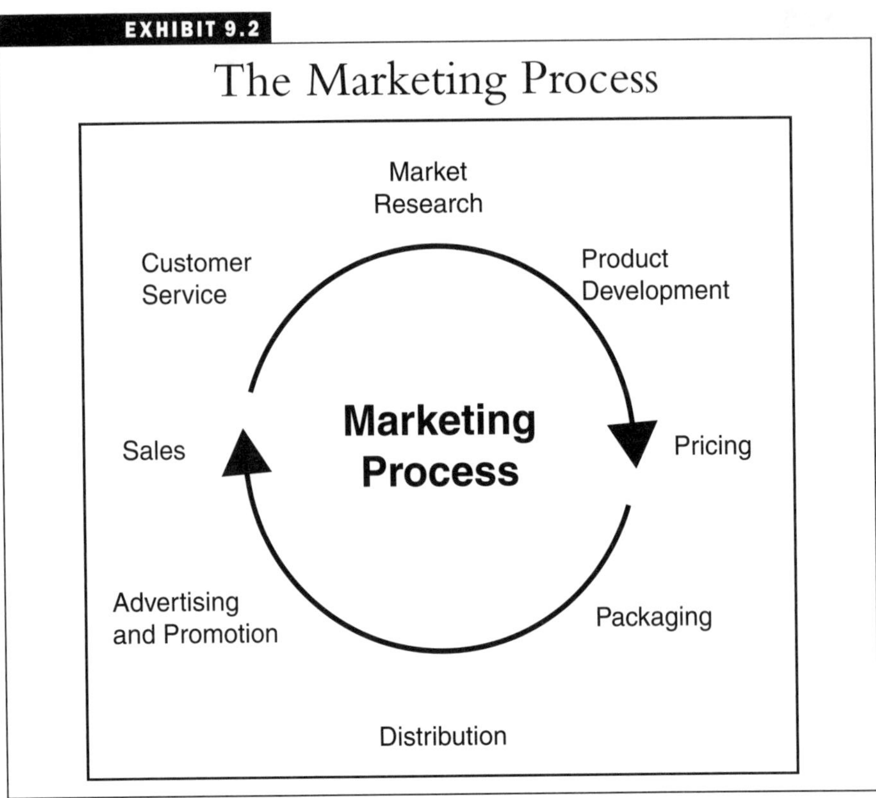

Selling is *not* a substitute for marketing, rather selling is part of the marketing process and an important way to communicate the marketing message. Many businesses try to go straight to the ask-for-the-order part of the marketing process, skipping over marketing steps such as:

- Market research
- Product development
- Competitive studies
- Distribution management

Sales, advertising, publicity, promotions, direct mail, and trade shows are all important ways of communicating with your prospective customers. But before you communicate, you need to know whom you're talking to, what they want to buy, and what you need to say to motivate their buying decision.

Marketing Plan

All businesses, large and small, must follow the same process to develop a marketing plan. They must:

- Conduct research.
- Set a goal, objectives, and strategies.
- Develop an implementation program.
- Develop a budget.

Information gained from research provides the background necessary to set goals, objectives, and strategies. A few definitions are in order.

- **Goal** The overall sales or business target.
- **Objective** States a specific, measurable means to achieve a goal.
- **Strategy** A plan of action that details the actions necessary to achieve a marketing objective.

From that research you can set the goals, define the objectives and plan the strategy for your marketing plan. Next, you can develop an implementation program and budget.

What is a marketing plan? It can be defined as an outline of a program designed to accomplish a business goal. Start the process of developing a marketing plan by gathering information about the customer, market, product, and competition. See Table 9.1 for some questions to ask. The answers to the research questions help establish marketing goals and objectives.

TABLE 9.1

Types of Research Questions to Ask

Information Type	Question
Customer	Which customers are profitable and which customers aren't?
	How can you get more business—and profits—from existing customers?
Market	What percentage of your market do you currently serve, and how can that be increased?
	What new market trends present you with growth opportunities or threats?
Product	What new products or services would help you win new customers, retain current customers, and gain more business from all customers?
Competition	Are your competitors making changes that will create marketing opportunities or threats?

TABLE 9.2

Sample Goals and Objectives

Goal	Objectives
Increase profits from banking services by 5 percent.	Increase interest income by 10 percent.
	Increase the number of customers with multiple accounts by 5 percent.
Create a new financial investments product line that contributes 2 percent of gross income.	Sell one new investment product to 50 percent of the most profitable customers.
	Attract 15 new customers who fit the most profitable customer profile with the financial investments product line.
Create a new insurance product line that contributes 5 percent of gross income.	Sell one new insurance product to 40 percent of current customers.
	Attract 100 new customers with the insurance product line.

Objectives state specific, measurable ways a goal will be achieved See Table 9.2 for sample goals and objectives. The objectives quantify results necessary for goal achievement. In other words, objectives define the major ways the goal will be achieved. The goal is the overall sales or business target. It is the purpose of the marketing plan.

The *marketing strategy* is the part of the marketing plan that details the steps necessary to achieve a marketing objective.

A strategy is how a business plans to achieve each marketing objective. In order to be effective, strategies must be achievable, action oriented, and flexible to respond to changes in economic conditions and market opportunities.

In a financial services company, an objective may be to increase its banking product line by increasing the number of customers with multiple accounts by 5 percent.

Every financial services company needs a game plan to achieve its objectives. It might develop these strategies:

- *Product development strategy.* Research and develop an umbrella account, a multiple account club, or other incentive programs to grow the number of current and new customer accounts.
- *Pricing strategy.* Research and develop a fee structure to insure profitability and competitive advantage for the new product.
- *Distribution strategy.* Research and develop a partnership with high-traffic retail organizations to gain visibility and promote the convenience aspect and other features of the new product.
- *Sales strategy.* Identify low-profit, single-account customers as primary targets for the new product. Research and develop a staff incentive program to reward sales.
- *Communications strategy.* Develop advertising, a statement stuffer, and in-branch displays to promote the new product.

Every marketer needs to balance four basic marketing decisions when crafting a marketing plan. The *Four Ps of the Marketing Mix* are:

1. *Product.* What are we selling?
2. *Place (or distribution).* How do we get the product to our customer?
3. *Price.* How much do we charge?
4. *Promotion.* How do we communicate our product and its advantages?

Customers: The Reason for Being in Business

To spend marketing money wisely, businesses must know as much as possible about the target customer. Without knowledge of the customer, marketing messages are shots in the dark.

- You can save time and money by focusing efforts on the customer groups most likely to purchase your product or service. Effective marketing messages appeal to the target customer's wants and needs and motivate target prospects to become customers.

Getting to Know the Customer

Three types of information are used to identify customers: geographics, demographics, and psychographics. Each of these information types plays a different role in customer identification.

Geographics identify customers by regions, counties, states, ZIP code areas, and census tracts to define where customers live and work.

Good marketers use geographics to help direct their marketing efforts. They start by talking to customers where their bank already has the greatest geographical advantage, for example, because they are the oldest or largest bank in a particular geographical area, then look for new geographical areas to develop after most of the prospects have become customers. (In other words, they have saturated the market.)

Knowing where your customers are (geographics) is just part of the puzzle. You need to narrow your target through demographic facts about your customers.

Demographics play an important role as well; they identify customers by facts such as age, gender, race, education, marital status, income, household size, and profession.

Two of the ways to gather personal data about your customers are to:

1. *Create a customer profile chart for each major product line.* Work with management and frontline staff to develop a best-guess profile of your current customers.
2. *Ask your customers questions.* Present questions indirectly by including them in surveys or questionnaires, or by incorporating them into contest forms.

Once you know where your customers are (geographics) and statistical facts about who they are (demographics), you are ready to wisely select the media to reach them.

Psychographics will help you do this; identify customers based on personal characteristics such as attitudes, beliefs, values, and lifestyles.

Until you know something about their attitudes and values (psychographics), you really don't know what to say to influence their decisions to buy from you. Customers demonstrate their attitudes and values when they make a purchase. Take a look at some examples of these factors:

Buying patterns	Price-sensitive
	Emotional
	Impulsive
Nature of the purchase	Loyal/repeat customer
	Promotion/price buyer
Competitive relationships	Competitive brands used by customer
Distribution channel	Mail
	Internet
	Off-premise outlet
	Referral

TABLE 9.3

Customer Psychographics for Your Products

	Buying Patterns	Nature of Purchase	Competitive Relation-ships	Distribution Channel
Product example	Price-sensitive Emotional Impulsive	Loyal/repeat customer Promotion/price buyer	Competitive brands used by customer	Mail Internet Off-premise outlet Referral
Product #1				
Product #2				

Use Table 9.3 to determine customer psychographics for your products.

Chart Instructions

1. List every major product you offer down one side.
2. List factors of customer behavior across the top.
3. Fill in the blanks starting with guesswork, then move to formal customer research (including focus groups) to determine *how* and *why* your customers buy.

Prospects, Customers, and Consumers

A *prospect* is a potential customer. A prospect is someone who fits the profile of a customer but who hasn't yet purchased your product or service.

A *customer* is a purchaser of your product or service.

A *consumer* is the person who actually uses your product or service. The consumer may or may not be the person who makes the purchase (i.e., the customer).

An *influencer* is the person who steers the buying decision.

Before spending money on advertising, a marketer should know everything there is to know about the profile of the prospective customer. Then the marketer should work to direct each and every communication dollar only at people who fit that description.

Your prospective customer:

- Resembles the demographic and psychographic profile of your current best customers
- Has wants or needs for the kinds of products you are offering
- Can easily access your business, either physically or via mail or Internet delivery services
- Has the ability and inclination to purchase the product

Converting prospects to customers is a four-step process.

1. *Awareness.* Make a first impression and inform the prospect about your business and your product.
2. *Interest.* Develop the prospect's interest in your business and your product.
3. *Desire.* Create desire to lead the prospect either to make a purchase or to get more information.
4. *Decision.* Lead the prospect to the buying decision based on product availability, proper pricing, a motivating offer, and so on.

The conversion process can be immediate or take place over time, depending on:

- Reputation of your business
- Nature of the product
- Price

Prospects can be converted to customers through a single marketing communication or over a period of time through extended marketing efforts.

- Prospects are turned into customers through efforts of the marketing department, but the entire organization must work to retain customers once they're on board. Everyone in an organization must work to keep customers, increase the volume of sales from existing customers, and develop new customers by turning current customers into referral sources.

Customer Economics

TIPS AND TECHNIQUES

Marketing Rule of Thumb

The cost of *getting* a customer is five times the cost of *keeping* a customer.

Question: Why did a customer leave?

Easy answer:	"We're too expensive."
Real reason:	"The customer received greater service and satisfaction elsewhere."

Monitor customer satisfaction levels by honestly evaluating how your business stacks up against the competition. But don't make the mistake of thinking all customers are equal. They are not.

Let's look at that theory by going back in time. A nineteenth-century economist named Vilfredo Pareto developed the theory that some customers are simply more valuable than others. All customers are important, but some are more likely to result in greater sales, greater profit, and better referrals.

IN THE REAL WORLD

Pareto's Law

20 percent of customers account for 80 percent of sales.

80 percent of the problems will come from 20 percent of the customers.

Give the bulk of your attention to the 20 percent of customers who account for the majority of your sales and profits. Plan your marketing efforts to attract more customers just like them.

Don't ignore the 20 percent of your clientele that has 80 percent of the problems, however. There are important lessons to be learned from their complaints and comments.

Customers don't buy products. Customers buy satisfaction and the fulfillment of needs or desires. When you communicate with a prospective customer, don't think about your product or service. Think primarily about your customer's needs or desires. Pinpoint your customer's wants and needs. Use the knowledge to create products and to communicate messages that speak directly to the desires your customer is trying to satisfy.

Market Share and Customer Share

Market share and customer share are important indicators of the success of a marketing plan:

- **Market share** The percentage of all sales in a market category captured by a business.
- **Customer share** The portion (that a business captures) of all the money that a *customer* spends in his or her market category.

Your market share is your slice of the business pie. It is the portion of all sales in your market category that are captured by your business. It is important to gather a sense of your market share to help:

- Assess your competitive rank.
- Monitor the growth of your business in relation to the growth of the total market.

Companies base their market share calculations on different types of data. Large companies use data gathered through major research efforts. Small companies employ data from annual reports of competitors, local economic development offices, business associations, and other resources.

To calculate market share, divide your share by the total market:

Your market share ÷ Total market

Market share can be calculated based on a variety of measures, such as:

- Total number of households
- Total dollars on deposit at financial institutions

Knowing and watching your market share will help you set goals that will lead to business growth.

To increase market share, you need to increase your customer satisfaction levels. Not only will that help attract new customers; it also will help you retain the valuable customers you currently serve.

Find areas where your business excels over your competition and emphasize those attributes in your marketing efforts. Take an honest look at the areas where your competition has an edge, and think about how you can close the gap. Continuous service improvements will help you keep and win customers.

Market *saturation* is when a business has achieved sales from an extraordinarily high percentage of all potential customers in its market area. The reality of the competitive marketplace makes it highly unlikely that a business will ever achieve sales to *all* of its potential customers. If a company sees its market share climb to a very high percentage, it should celebrate—and then it should start looking for other ways to grow its business. Be reasonable in your market share expectations. Remember that even the leading brands in the world do not enjoy anywhere near 100 percent market share.

Be reasonable in your market share expectations. Remember that even the leading brands in the world do not enjoy anywhere near 100 percent market share.

Some market share leaders lose when it comes to profitability because they sacrifice profits to "buy" market share. When a business relies heavily on low pricing, that business increases market share at the expense of profit and at the even greater expense of customer dedication. Typically when price is used to attract customers, the customers it attracts are not loyal; rather these customers buy from the lowest bidder.

Customer share can also be used to assess the success of a marketing plan. Say a customer of Financial Institution A also does business with Financial Institution B and Financial Institution C.

If the customer's business is split equally among the three banks, then we could say that each financial institution has a 33 percent share of that customer's business:

$$1 \div 3 = .33 = 33 \text{ percent}$$

Gathering customer share information can reveal ways that customers use your products. For example, various financial services institutions may discover:

- A high percentage of checking account customers also keep certificates of deposit and safe deposit boxes.
- Most customers keep car and home insurance with the same company.
- A high percentage of customers keep retirement accounts and short-term investment accounts at the same company.

Information on customer share can suggest product offerings to solidify customer relationships. For example, financial services institutions may:

- Bundle checking accounts, certificates of deposit, and safe deposit boxes as a product.

- Give discounts for home insurance if a customer buys car insurance.
- Charge a lower management fee for multiple investment accounts.

Increasing your "share of customer" requires:

- A commitment to product and service quality
- An organization-wide dedication to make each customer a customer for life

If you want to earn a greater share of customer:

- Earn your customers' commitment to your business.
- Pay attention to your customers.
- Work to earn and win a greater share of their business.
- Listen to their wants and needs.
- Solve their problems.
- Build long-term relationships.
- Increase the business you do with customers by finding ways to satisfy more of their needs with more of your products.

The Product: Price and Value

To grow your market share, you need to offer the right products to the right prospective customers.

Pricing decisions are an important part of the product mix. These decisions start with research questions that ask what the customer is willing to pay and what competitors are charging. Today's value-conscious consumers will likely value a low price for high-volume products and high quality for large, long-term purchases. The importance of competitive pricing can be overcome only by a product or service that offers something extra and special for the higher price.

Product strategies stem from decisions on product positioning and branding. Most marketers agree that product positioning is the most important step a business can take in the marketing process.

Ultimately, businesses must remember that customers buy satisfaction from a product, not a product on its own.

Product Decisions

As part of the marketing process, every business needs to periodically review its product mix to be sure it is making the right products and marketing them to the right customers (see Exhibit 9.3).

A periodic product review determines whether:

- Existing products fit existing customers.
- New products should be introduced to existing customers.
- Existing products can attract new customers.
- New products should be introduced to attract new customers.

The results of the periodic product review will help you determine:

- What products to market
- How to market those products

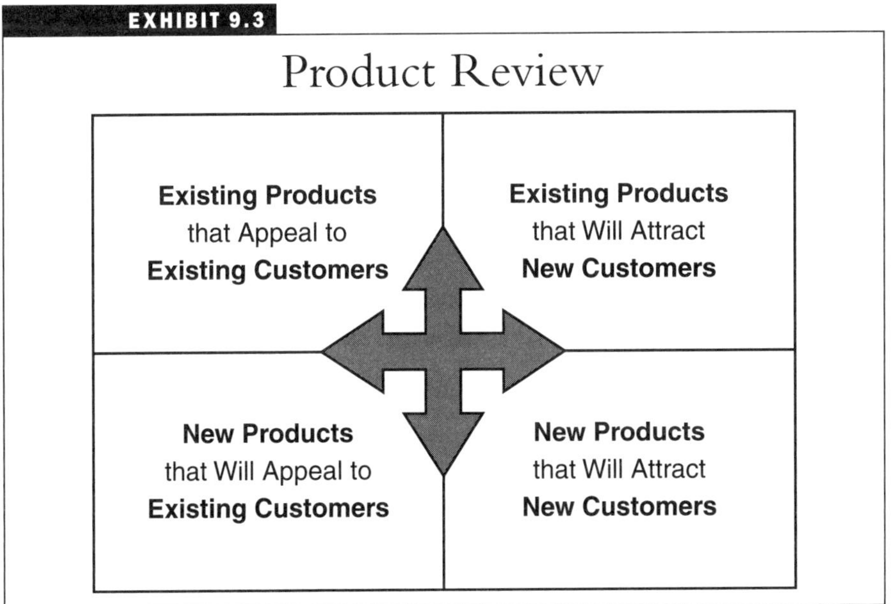

To target new customers, start with a product review to see which of your current products are capable of drawing new customers into your business. You may conclude that to attract new customers, you need to:

- Create a new product.
- Alter an existing product by making it more appealing and/or competitive.

Product Development

Continuous monitoring of products helps to ensure that they are profitable and in line with market demand. Product development takes research, intelligence, and discipline. Be willing to brainstorm. Create lots of ideas, research them, and then be selective.

Back your choices all the way: with research, development, promotions, advertising, and the complete confidence that comes from a successful product development effort.

When products become old and tired, revitalize them or retire them. Each of these questions should be answered before a new product is approved:

- What current product can we update or enhance?
- What new product idea should we consider to provide new customer solutions?
- What market trends can we address?
- Do we have the human and capital resources to back this new product?
- Does this product have proven market potential?
- Does this new product already exist in the marketplace? If so, how will our version be different and better?
- Does this new product fit with our company objectives and existing product line?

A way to revitalize old products is to create product line extensions.

Product Line Extensions

A product line extension adds related products to a product mix. There are several questions to address when dealing with an extension. Does this new product fit in our line? Will our customers believe that our organization is capable of excelling in this new area? If not, are we willing to invest the funds necessary to help convince them that we have the expertise?

Product Life Cycle

The product life cycle begins with product development and proceeds until the product reaches its market maturity, after which time its sales growth rate slows and profits decrease (see Exhibit 9.4).

When a product reaches maturity, a business has several choices:

- Abandon the product in favor of new products that better meet product wants and needs.
- Maintain the product with minor marketing investment and minor sales and profit expectations.

EXHIBIT 9.4

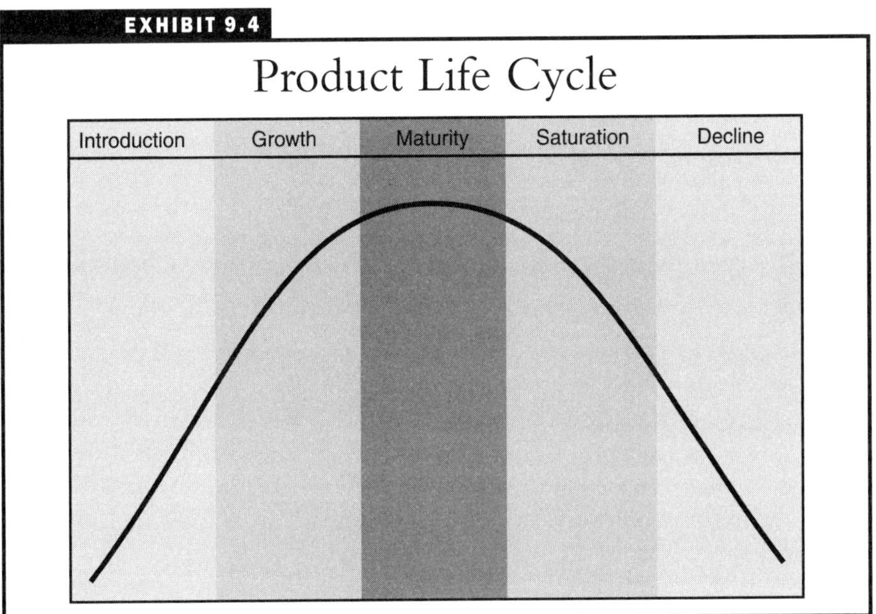

- Renew the product by reinventing its technology, design, usage, or target market.

Pricing Decisions

Regarding pricing, it's important to start with research by asking:

- What is your customer willing and able to spend?
- What are your competitors charging?

The more value the customer perceives in your product or brand, the more he or she will be willing to spend.

Every customer seeks value from purchasing decisions. Where does value come from? Value is not a product feature. Value is the customer's perception of his or her purchase. Value can come from price or quality, depending on the type of purchase:

You can't charge more than everyone else unless you offer the customer something extra and special for the higher price, such as:

- Extraordinary level of service
- Lifetime guarantee
- Unchallenged safety or quality attribute
- Some other characteristic that makes your higher purchase price acceptable

To succeed, you don't have to have the lowest price. Customers are willing to pay a higher price for greater value. *If* you have the highest price, then you must also have the highest perceived value. The equation is simple: The highest-priced product must have the highest perceived value.

Too often, struggling businesses believe that lower prices are the answer to increasing business. Lower prices simply lower your margins, *unless* they significantly increase your volume at the same time.

If you have a:

- *Higher price,* customers must be helped to understand the features that add value so they will be willing to pay a premium to do business with you.
- *Lower price,* business systems that handle advertising, promotion, and distribution must be able to manage higher volume.

Price is rarely, if ever, the only reason that businesses lose customers.

Developing Product Strategies

Each product must have a marketing strategy that is based on the four Ps: product, price, promotion, and place (or distribution). Decisions about the four Ps will lead to product positioning and branding. Most marketers agree that product positioning is the most important step a business can take in the marketing process. In marketing, *positioning* means determining the appropriate market niche for the product.

Marketers must seek answers to questions that will help them determine:

- The true nature of their business
- Their product's strengths and weaknesses
- Their competitors' strengths and weaknesses
- The wants and needs of their target market

The process of determining your product's positioning includes:

- Evaluating your product
- Analyzing the evaluation results
- Establishing a position

Businesses determine the unoccupied market niche for a product only after completing this process. When evaluating your product, ask yourself these questions:

Does this product offer customers a benefit that they really want? If not, can you create the need or desire?

Is the product unique or at least difficult to copy?

Is the product compatible with the trends of the economy and market?

The answers to these questions will help you to understand your product's *brand*. What is a brand? It is an identity that communicates a promise about the benefits of a product. For example:

Unique	**Predictable**
7-Up as the "uncola"	Your Roots financial institution becomes known as "the hometown financial partner"

Most people think of brands as registered trademarks. In fact, more than a million brands are trademarked in America. But you don't need a trademark to have a brand.

A brand is simply a word or a symbol conveying a set of characteristics that influence how the market thinks about and makes decisions regarding a company's products. You can create brand identification using:

- Product names
- Logos
- Symbols
- Colors
- Type fonts
- Product design
- Package design

You'll hear marketers rant and rave over graphic consistency, begging everyone in the organization to use the logo properly:

- In the right color
- With the right type font

- In designs that are consistent with all other communications

Businesses Think They Sell Products	Customers Think They Buy Satisfaction
Investment services	Hope for a nest egg for retirement
Cars	Reliable, safe transportation
Sewing machines	Creative tool

Businesses must:

- Look long and hard at why their customers buy.
- Think of all the alternatives that could meet that same desire.
- Position their offering as the very best choice to fulfill the customer's underlying need.

Competition

Competition is a basic tenet of the free enterprise system.

Competition versus Monopoly

Competition is the struggle among businesses for customers and sales. *Monopoly* is exclusive control by a single company over production and/or sale of a product.

Competition benefits the marketplace in many ways:

- It forces businesses to produce higher-quality products at reasonable prices.
- It stimulates product improvements and innovations.
- It results in a wider selection of goods and services.
- It motivates companies to seek production, service, cost, and delivery efficiencies.

Most businesses compete for customers by emphasizing either price or nonprice attributes. Businesses that emphasize price must aim to offset low profit margins with high sales volume. Businesses that aim to charge a higher price must compete based on nonpricing benefits, including:

- Quality
- Service
- Location
- Reputation
- Uniqueness of product
- Customer convenience

As our society has grown increasingly value oriented, more companies try to offer both low prices and favorable nonprice attributes. Price-oriented companies tout quality and service, while quality-oriented companies tout discounted prices. The customers' value orientation blurs the lines between price and nonprice strategies.

Competition may not be obvious. It may not even be direct. But it is always there. The sooner you identify and plan for these competitors, the better.

Products or offerings similar to yours that the customer thinks of as substitutes for your products are your *direct competitors*. Products or offerings that satisfy the same customer needs as you do, but do it through very different methods, are your *indirect competitors*. Products or offerings that are alternative solutions to your offered products or services are *hidden competitors*. Hidden competitors are the hardest to recognize.

Table 9.4 is an example of how to describe a financial institution's competition for savings accounts. Use Table 9.5 to get a sense of how you compare with your competitors.

On an annual or regular basis, every business should ask:

- With whom do we really compete?
- How can we move up the competitive ladder?

TABLE 9.4

Competitive Analysis

What You Sell	Direct Competitors	Indirect Competitors	Hidden Competitors
Savings accounts	Bank A	Life insurance	Pay bills
	Credit Union B	Mutual funds	$$ under mattress
	Savings & Loan C	Precious metals	Lottery tickets

- Do we compete with the most reputable, successful businesses in our market arena or with the second-string players?
- Do people think of us as among the best or as a good second choice?
- Who is our actual current competition? To whom are we currently losing business?
- How can we move up the competitive ladder?
- If we're not considered among the most reputable, successful businesses in our market arena, what would it take to become so?
- Do the strongest businesses in our competitive arena consider our business a competitive threat? If not, what would it take to become a stronger competitive force?

TABLE 9.5

Strengths and Weaknesses vs. Competition

Competitors	Strengths When Compared to Your Business	Weaknesses When Compared to Your Business	What Your Business Could Do to Win Their Customers Over
Competitor A			
Competitor B			
Competitor C			
Competitor D			

Getting the Word Out: Advertising

Types of Advertising

- **Advertising** A means of informing that persuades a prospect to consider the purchase of a product.

Advertising is used to protect market share and avoid the profit erosion that results from overemphasis on pricing. There are two main categories of advertising:

1. Institutional
2. Promotional

Institutional and promotional advertising have different goals.

Institutional advertising is designed to create a favorable impression and goodwill toward a business. Institutional ads prompt the market to see the advertiser as:

- An important contributor to the good of the community
- A leader in areas such as health, environment, education, or other causes that are important to the market and meaningful to the advertiser

Institutional advertising is designed and placed with the primary purpose of increasing sales.

Promotional advertising aims to:

- Create awareness and interest in the advertiser's product.
- Explain product features and benefits.
- Describe how and where to purchase the product.
- Call for buyer action.

Don't run an institutional ad when you need the results that only a promotional ad will deliver.

Media Outlets

"Media" can be defined as all means used to convey messages to the public. There are four primary categories of media:

1. Print
2. Broadcast
3. Specialty
4. New

Print Media. Print media includes all written forms of communication, such as:

- Newspapers
- Magazines
- Direct mail
- Outdoor ads and signage
- Directories

Newspapers

For a relatively low investment in placement and production costs and a short lead time, newspapers offer advertisers:

- A large readership
- A high level of interest and involvement by readers
- Clearly defined geographical or interest areas

Magazines

Magazine advertising requires significant advance planning. Often ad materials must be prepared months before the publication is sent to consumers. Magazines offer:

- Easily defined reader characteristics and high reader involvement

- High-quality imagery
- A longer life span than many other forms of media

Magazines are generally divided into two groups:

1. Consumer magazines read for personal pleasure or interest
2. Business or trade magazines read by those with particular interest in a specialty field

Direct Mail

Direct mail includes all media vehicles sent to prospective customers directly by advertisers, including:

- Newsletters
- Catalogs
- Coupons
- Samplers
- Circulars
- Invitations
- Statement stuffers

Direct mail is a highly targeted but fairly costly form of media. Each mailing requires the production of the piece to be mailed, plus the cost of postage. Direct offers flexibility in timing, since the advertiser can choose the mail date. The expected response rate is between 1 and 2 percent of all recipients.

Direct mail has a negative "junk mail" image.

Outdoor Advertising and Signage

From site signage to highway billboards, outdoor advertising is a means of achieving visibility and name recognition on a regular, repeated basis.

- *Signage* is often limited to the name of a business, usually accompanied by its logo and occasionally by a slogan or tagline.
- *Outdoor boards* are limited to a short selling message (not exceeding seven words) to allow drivers to comprehend it.
- *Transit ads* are posted on public transportation facilities and vehicles, an economical means to reach a captive, usually urban audience

Directories

A visible form of directory advertising is the yellow pages of telephone books.

Broadcast Media. Broadcast media, such as radio and television, have extensive penetration. Advertising on broadcast media is:

- Expensive
- Usually highly effective

Broadcast media offer market demographics so that businesses can select the media most likely to reach their target market.

When several stations in a geographical area cover the same demographic group, advertisers will often buy time on multiple channels to increase target market coverage.

- Commercials or spots
- Advertisements run on broadcast media

Radio

Radio advertisements can be highly targeted to a particular audience so advertisers can select their audience based on age or interests. Radio ads:

- Can be produced quickly, so ads can be on the air within hours of their completion.

- Require repetition to be effective; therefore, each ad plan requires numerous airings of the same message.
- Require an entertaining or provocative message to hold listeners' attention.

To use radio time effectively, an advertiser must:

- Determine which stations reach the target market.
- Buy time for the times of day when those listeners are tuned in.
- Create an ad capable of drawing the listeners' interest and action.
- Purchase an advertising package large enough to ensure that a high percentage of target listeners hear the message several times during the advertising period.

Television

Television allows an advertiser to combine sound, art, motion, and color to deliver an ad message into the prospective customer's home during leisure hours. Television:

- Is highly believable.
- Reaches a mass audience but can be targeted to viewers with specific interests.
- Involves the highest costs of all media ads; in most cases, multiple airings are necessary.

To place television ads, you need to understand:

- *Spot buys.* These ads are purchased to air throughout the signal area of local stations. The ads may air during a network program; they will be viewed only within the market area of the local channel.
- *Network buys.* These are ads purchased to air over the entire network. They cost hundreds of thousands of dollars, depending on

the visibility and time slot of the selected program in which the ads are to air.

- *Gross Point Rating.* The GRP is defined as 1 percent of televisions in a market area. The rule of thumb for purchasing television ads is 100 to 150 GRPs of monthly viewership.

Specialty Media. Specialty media are imprinted with an advertiser's name and promotional message. Some examples include:

- Matchbooks
- Pens
- Memo pads
- Key chains
- License plate holders
- Calendars

Specialty media promotions have these limitations:

- Must be useful to be successful
- Must be well designed, and carry a name and meaningful message
- Are given to individuals who may never be prospective customers
- Can dilute an advertiser's brand image if not carefully designed and managed

Be careful that the items are consistent with the overall image of the advertiser, or they can do as much harm as good.

New Media. Innovation is thought by many to be the advertising key in the twenty-first century. From sports arena electronic signage to Internet banners and web pages, technology increasingly presents new advertising opportunities. Many advertising agencies have departments devoted to the assessment and selection of new media. They can assist clients as they enter the world of high-tech media advertising. New media marketing not only offers more ways for advertisers and consumers to interact, it has created new ways to track and report on that interaction. Specifically, new media campaigns can be focused around a direct call to action through virtual point-of-purchase opportunities and opt-in lead generation. In addition, new media marketing has an intrinsic capacity that allows advertisers to reach unintended but highly targeted end users.

Look also to the expertise provided by web-based marketing specialists. From web site design to link building and search engine optimization, technology is providing an opportunity for unlimited innovation.

Sales and Promotional Materials

In addition to paid media advertising, businesses promote their messages through a wide range of sales and promotional materials, including:

- Brochures and printed sales materials
- Events
- Personal contacts
- Personal letters
- Product packaging
- Point-of-purchase and in-store displays
- Premium offers
- Promotions
- Public relations
- Publicity
- Sales presentations
- Seminars
- Specialty offers (T-shirts, pens, etc.)

- Telemarketing
- Trade shows

Plan Your Advertising

Make precious advertising dollars count by knowing your prospective customer.

Know your customer. Understand:

- Which media reach your customers
- What customers need to know about your product or service
- What will motivate customers to make the purchasing decision
- What you want your ad to achieve

You wouldn't believe how many advertisers fault an ad for "not making the phone ring" when, on review, the ad offered no reason for the prospective customer to pick up the phone.

To develop and place advertising, marketers use:

- Advertising agencies
- Media representatives
- Printing company representatives
- Other advertising suppliers

Many marketers hire professional advertising skills on an as-needed hourly basis rather than use internal staff. Professional advertising agencies provide:

- Creative thinking
- Competent media knowledge
- Commercial and production knowledge
- Understanding of consumer attitudes and market trends
- Market, industry, and product experience
- Initiative and enthusiasm

Good marketers consider media sales offers carefully by:

- Reviewing the written details and advantages of offers
- Demanding time to weigh the benefits of the offer against the defined aims of the established marketing and advertising plans

Public Relations and Publicity

Public Relations

Public relations activities supplement the marketing plan by creating a positive image of the company. Activities such as community relations, media relations, and publicity are undertaken to create goodwill toward a business and its products.

Public relations programs generate news and goodwill for a company in a target market area through events, sponsorships, community and charitable activities, and media placements. Public relations activities include:

- Grand openings
- Product launches
- Corporate media interviews with key executives and board members
- Corporate-sponsored community activities
- Charitable activities, including donations of time and funds

Well-designed public relations activities:

- Build a company's good reputation.
- Spread accurate information about a company through unpaid news coverage.
- Build meaningful and useful relationships with key contacts in government and industry.

- Condition prospective customers to expect quality products and actions from the company.

Publicity

The primary purpose of publicity is to build a positive image for a company. Publicity is the result of achieving news coverage about a company and its people and products in newspapers, magazines, newsletters, radio, television, and other types of media. Publicity is about news. It's not intended to build sales in particular but rather to create awareness and goodwill for a business.

Some businesses think publicity is free. That's partially true, because the stories are run or aired without any media charges. However, there are costs—in time, effort, and planning—to stage events and to package stories so the media can easily turn them into news articles or features.

Publicity tools include:

- *Press conferences.* Media representatives are invited to these meetings organized by a business or organization to hear an announcement about a newsworthy event.
- *Press kits.* Press kits include packets of information, such as:
  - Background information
  - News releases
  - Illustrations or photos of a company, product, or person
- *News releases.* News releases are stories written for distribution to the media that summarize a newsworthy event or situation and focus on information about the company's employees, operations, products, or philosophy.

Instead of viewing publicity as "free," view it as a highly valuable and credible way to have news about your company presented by a third-party, objective voice.

Summary

The marketing process links the efforts of businesses to produce and sell products that meet the desires of their customers. When marketing is strong, you know what you're selling, whom you're up against, and what threats or opportunities are on the business horizon. A good marketer knows what the customer wants and needs and tailors products, services, and messages in order to build a win-win buyer–seller relationship. Sales is not a substitute for the marketing process. When businesses leapfrog to sales, they often end up struggling to sell products that competitors already offer and customers don't really want. Often these businesses do not have a carefully researched market position.

All businesses must follow the same process to develop a marketing plan: conduct research, set a goal including objectives and strategies, develop an implementation program, and develop a budget. The Four Ps of the Marketing Mix are product, place, price and promotion.

To spend marketing dollars wisely, it's important to know as much as possible about the target customer. Customer-profiling information used to determine the marketing mix includes geographics, demographics, and psychographics.

There's a four-step process to follow in using marketing to convert prospects to customers: awareness, interest, desire, and decision. The conversion process can be immediate or take place over time. However, the cost of converting a prospect to a customer is five times the cost of keeping a customer.

Market share is your slice of the business pie. To increase market share, you need to increase your customer satisfaction levels and offer the right products to the right prospective customers. As part of the marketing process, every bank should review its product mix to determine whether existing products fit customers, new products should be introduced to customers, existing products can attract new customers, and new products should be introduced to attract new customers. This review helps determine what products to market and how to market them.

Summary

Continuous monitoring of products helps ensure that products are profitable and in line with market demand. The product life cycle begins with product development and proceeds until the product meets market maturity, after which time sales growth rate slows and profits decrease.

Brand is an identity that communicates a promise about the benefits of the product. Consistency builds brands, which is why marketers demand graphic consistency.

Advertising also is a critical component of any marketing program. There are two main categories of advertising: institutional and promotional. Institutional advertising is designed to create a favorable impression and goodwill toward a business. Promotional advertising is designed and placed with the primary purpose of increasing sales.

CHAPTER 10

Customer Service: The Key Ingredient

After reading this chapter, you will be able to:

- Define the elements of good customer service.
- Understand the importance of a learning organization.
- Recognize, prepare for, and successfully service the challenging customer.
- Follow up and follow through with customers and colleagues.

Customer Service

What Is Customer Service?

Customer service is defined in many ways. Still, a satisfied customer is always the result of successful customer service.

In addition to the quantifiable costs and benefits associated with improved customer service, by undertaking a customer service initiative, your company can expect increases in general goodwill and workforce satisfaction.

You can identify good customer service by its results. Good customer service results in a satisfied customer who would return for more services or recommend your financial services company to others.

One of the most important activities in a customer service initiative is defining what the word *customer* means in your workgroup. Many customers are easy to identify: They walk through the door and ask for service. But other types of customers are more difficult to see as customers. For instance, if you work in the human resources department, your customers are all of the employees of the company, and perhaps the hiring managers.

Only terminology separates the customer who walks through the door and the one who works at the desk next to you. *Internal* customers work within your company. *External* customers walk through the door of your company.

A few other elements and terms you may encounter as you strive to improve your company's customer service are *process*, *quality*, and *expectation*. Process includes the steps required to deliver a service to an internal or external customer. Quality is associated with the service level that meets the customer's requirements. Finally, expectation is the service level a customer anticipates before the service is delivered.

Another important concept related to the benefit of excellent customer service is called the *lifetime value* of a customer. The lifetime value of a customer is equal to the sum of the revenue created by sales of services to that customer. For example, the lifetime value of an insurance customer is the total of all premiums paid by the customer over the time the customer does business with the insurance company. In view of this computation of value, you can see that losing the customer over poor customer service during a claim for a minor fender-bender would be a mistake and a losing proposition for the insurance company.

It is commonly believed that a dissatisfied customer will tell 10 people about his or her experience. Thus, the negative publicity created by a disgruntled customer can be substantial, and it can blunt or even negate the advertising and marketing efforts a financial services company undertakes.

Another intangible related to customer service is the fact that, in general, employees who are fulfilled and energized by their work create more value for a company and stay at the company longer.

Consider these questions:

- How many employees did your call center lose last year because they *couldn't tolerate dealing with unhappy customers* any more?
- How many employees left to take positions that would require less *public interaction*?
- What is the *turnover rate* among your tellers?

The cost to recruit and train each of those replacements is substantial, not to mention the drain on organizational knowledge that occurs when a seasoned employee leaves.

The first step of an effective customer service initiative is to determine exactly the needs and wants of the customer. Of course, it is impossible to survey each and every one of your customers to determine each and every one of their needs and wants. However, you can focus strategically on customers who have the highest lifetime value to your company and comprise the largest categories among your customer base. While anecdotal information might serve a useful purpose in a needs assessment, the best instruments gather quantifiable information.

The most powerful customer service programs are started and supported at the top executive levels. If you consider that some innovative companies now draw their organizational charts upside-down (showing how management supports frontline workers), then those programs grow from the bottom up.

Even without support from the national office or chief executive of your company, you can undertake a customer service initiative. These initiatives, in which members of a single department or function work together, are commonly called *workgroup projects*. These workgroup efforts occur in many forms, informally and formally, in branch offices, specific departments, and within groups of employees.

A specific and popular form of workgroup project is called the *quality circle*. The quality circle was introduced in Japanese manufacturing by Kaoru Ishikawa in the early 1960s. At that time, the work of the quality circle centered on reducing product defects and improving production processes. However, quality circles have spread in use and popularity and are now common in service companies as well.

A quality circle is a group of employees from the same function or department that meets regularly to discuss common issues, to improve processes, and to improve customer service. The circle may or may not have a coordinator or leader who is responsible for communicating:

- Management sponsors' direction to the circle
- The circle's findings and recommendations to upper management

The benefits of quality circles include employees who feel involved and invested in improving customer service and increased morale.

A quality team is composed of representatives from various operational areas of a company. Quality teams are especially effective at addressing issues that:

- Involve complicated procedures
- Affect primarily internal customers

Imagine that a financial planning firm wished to address customer service in an all-encompassing fashion, improving quality from the moment a customer called or walked into the office, to the next year when that same customer might have a Roth IRA question. The customer service initiative would have to improve the:

- Greeting given on the phone or by the receptionist
- Interaction with a financial planner
- Phone or mail follow-up to accomplish the goals of the meeting
- Periodic reporting to the client
- Channel through which that customer submits the Roth IRA question

This initiative might even predetermine that many clients of the firm will have questions about IRAs. A resulting decision may be made to write, design, and mail a client educational piece about various IRA options.

The initiative would require the participation and coordination of administrative staff, professional financial planners, service providers (some of whom might be external companies), and communications or marketing staff. Thus, this effort would require a multidisciplinary team of representatives from across the company.

Customer Service Techniques

Since the individual employees in your company are ultimately responsible for providing service to customers, giving them the authority necessary to solve customer problems is essential.

Service-level standards are an effective way to help both internal and external customers set expectations that your company can meet. These standards also provide ways to quantify whether service is being provided as planned. For example, the attorneys in your trust and estate group could include this sentence in their voice mail messages: "I will return your call by the end of the next business day." Thus, customers leaving a message will know what to *expect*. If they don't receive a return call on the day they call, they know they can expect one the next day.

These are examples of service-level standards in dealing with external customers; however, internal customers should also know what to expect in terms of service.

For example, a field agent with an insurance company should know exactly how many days it would take the central office to produce a policy rider. That agent could then provide better service to the external customer.

To know whether your customer service initiatives are working, you must also *measure the results*. One term closely related to measuring results is *return on investment* (ROI). ROI is the revenue or profit created by making an investment or expenditure. Because customer service projects typically involve expenditures of employee time, operating funds, and perhaps even expenditures on capital equipment such as computers to run specialized programs, companies are naturally concerned that those outlays create value. ROI will be used to help quantify the benefits your company can expect after making those expenditures.

Everyone probably has had the experience of a service person helping in spite of the fact that he or she had no authority to do so or was stretching company rules to help. We've also had the experience of a service person who could not solve a simple problem because he or she had no authority to do so. Your company's employees probably have had these experiences as well. As a result, they will do what they can to help customers if they are authorized to do so.

Your frontline employees know what the most common customer complaints are because they hear them everyday. They probably have some great ideas for solving those problems. An effective technique for individual empowerment is to gather information pertaining to customer complaints, create alternative solutions, and authorize your staff to make on-the-spot decisions to meet customer expectations. The most successful financial services companies place customers at the center of their customer service efforts. To create real improvement in customer service, the company must develop a service-focused culture throughout the company, including management/employee relationships. Additionally, management must seek and accept feedback from employees, and performance objectives should incorporate quantifiable service levels and problem resolution skills.

If employees feel that they are working side by side with their managers to achieve the common goal of customer satisfaction, they will rise to and exceed management's expectations. In a service-focused company, each objective in an employee's performance review will relate to customer service and service-level standards.

For example, if you determine that all high-end investment clients will receive a phone call from their personal banker each month, then a simple log sheet of customers and check-in calls can measure whether each personal banker has met that objective.

You might establish an objective stating that only a certain number of customers with complaints will call the branch manager before the customer's problem has been called to the manager's attention by a department supervisor. Of course, the success of this type of objective depends on your determination of the number of complaints that reached the manager before the customer service initiative and on an appropriate goal for reduction of this number.

Financial services companies are moving quickly to keep up with the customer expectation that more and more services will be provided at Internet sites. Individualized customer service remains important in online financial services, under the term *personalization*. In addition to sophisticated web site tools and personalization strategies, your company can utilize simpler and more familiar avenues to improve customer service, such as e-mail.

In the rush to transfer services to the Web, many companies forget just how beneficial some of the simplest customer service techniques can be. Strategies at personal points of contact, such as the phone and a teller window, can help solve customers' problems and let them know what services to expect.

The Learning Organization

At the beginning of your customer service initiative, you should plan to continue your efforts in successful cycles of change. Thus, you will need to make substantial allowances for employee training and ongoing education. Customer service projects do not end; they evolve. However, the customer service initiative that is launched and then left to die in employees' and managers' minds due to inaction is doomed to fail. The following activities, often called *continuous improvement*, are cyclical and should be ongoing:

- Needs assessments
- Employee training
- Integration into the performance process
- Outcomes measurement
- Feedback

In order to ensure continuous improvement, you need to follow up on any activities intended to create change and to continue assessing needs and gathering feedback when undertaking customer service initiatives.

Dealing with Challenging Customers

Despite doing everything you can to please your customers, there will be times when you are faced with customers who are unhappy. Understanding the cause of their displeasure will help you to serve all customers better.

Every customer comes to you with expectations, regardless of the situation. Knowing what customers expect and how to recognize and prepare yourself for a challenging customer allows you to meet and exceed their expectations and turn a difficult situation into one that wins customer loyalty.

It happens to everyone. You're moving as fast as you can to handle the long line of customers, when you look up and there is "the" customer. You know the one: the angry customer who is bent on ruining your day.

While some customers are unpleasant because of problems unrelated to you or your organization, there are also several other reasons people may act out when they come face to face with you. Some of these reasons might be:

- Nancy had to wait in a long line because two tellers are out sick and she's now late for work.
- Hank overdrew his account and he is positive it is the bank's error, even though you know it is not
- Ken is being charged software fees even though he canceled the service six months ago. Calls to customer service haven't resolved the problem, so he's coming into the bank and expects you to fix it *now*!
- Becky has moved but her checking account statements are going to her old address. She thinks you should have automatically changed the address since her home loan is also with your bank.

Customers may have a problem that they believe your organization doesn't want to solve, or it may be that the customer has made a mistake, which embarrasses him or her. Regardless of the root of the behavior, understand that you are the catalyst for the situation, probably not the cause of it.

When a customer comes to you angry and upset, you must first tend to his or her emotions. Challenging customers expect three things from you:

1. They want their problem heard.
2. They want an apology.
3. They want to have their problem solved.

Customers Want Their Problem Heard

Upset customers will begin to complain to you immediately. If you listen and pay attention to what they are telling you, you give validity to that problem, which will begin to calm the customers immediately. But if you appear to brush upset customers off, they will feel unimportant, and their anger and frustration will increase.

Once customers have voiced the problem, you should immediately acknowledge the problem. Apologize for the perceived wrong. Apologize for the situation or for the way the customers feel, if you cannot apologize for the problem. What's important is that customers hear the words "I'm sorry."

Finally, customers want the problem—whatever they perceive it to be—solved. You must be proactive in providing a solution. Customers are looking to you to solve the problem; approach them with a can-do attitude, and you'll diffuse the situation right away.

Often a situation with a frustrated customer escalates because you missed the warning signs that indicate a problem. People's body language often displays signs that will help you to spot a challenging customer and be prepared before you are confronted with their irritation.

Here are some indicators that there could be a problem:

- Reddened face
- Hunched shoulders
- Restlessness
- Nervousness

When you see these signs, prepare yourself for the challenge that you face pleasing a tough customer.

Greet the customer in a friendly tone of voice. Ask open-ended questions that lead to answers. For example, "How can I help you today?" is a better question than "Can I help you?" Avoid questions that can be answered with a simple "yes" or "no." If you can get the customer to talk to you, you stand a better chance of solving the problem.

Customers can tell when you are having a bad day or when their presence is an imposition on you. Prepare yourself for the challenging customer by always putting your best foot forward. Smile. It has been proven to improve your attitude.

Another way to prepare to please even the toughest customer is to expect them. Then make it a game to please even the most challenging person. Challenge yourself to make every customer happy, and you'll find that happiness to be infectious.

The worst thing you can do when faced with a difficult customer is to respond in an equally difficult manner. Maintaining a cool-as-a-cucumber demeanor when the customer is blaming you for all of the world's problems isn't easy. But if you understand where their anger comes from and use the right words combined with positive body language, you can maintain your cool and calm the customer, too.

Understanding why a customer is being difficult is the key to diffusing the situation. Customers don't get angry just because they can. There is usually an underlying reason for the anger. Anger is uncomfortable for anyone, and the response to anger is usually one of defense. You don't need to be defensive. The customer's anger is at the situation, not at you.

To learn what is causing customers' anger, listen to them. Then reflect or repeat what they are telling you. If you hear what customers are telling you, you will learn the cause of their anger. Then you can provide a solution that will diffuse that anger. *Negative language will only make a bad situation worse.*

Customers Want an Apology

Customers don't want to hear phrases like "I can't . . . ," "We don't . . . ," or "That's not . . . ." Each of those phrases tells the customer what *isn't* going to happen.

Telling customers what you *can't* do is certain to make them more angry or upset. Customers already know what is not being done; they don't need you to repeat it for them.

Knowing to avoid negative language is only half the battle. The other half is phrasing your words to have the best impact. If you know what not to say to the customer but don't know what you should say, then you'll be left with silence and an angry customer.

Rather than telling customers what you cannot do, try telling them what you *can* do. Explain what you are doing, so customers know that some action is being taken.

Get into the habit of using the phrase "What I *can* do is . . . ," then follow that phrase with a specific action designed to begin the solution process.

Psychologists say that about 93 percent of what we communicate is nonverbal. What you say, how you say it, and what your body language conveys can, at times, be extremely different things. Just as a customer can speak volumes without saying a word, so can you. The way you hold yourself, the look on your face, even the way you move can clue a customer in on your mood.

Your tone of voice should always be pleasant. Be sure to use inflections when you speak rather than speaking in a monotone. If you are slouched or hunched over, your body language tells customers that you really don't want to help. Stand straight, not slouched.

Nod and smile. If you're too tired to move, go home. Move with purpose, but not too quickly or too slowly. Quick movements usually signal nervousness. Slow movements can be read to mean you don't want to help.

Before any solution can be reached, both you and your customer must be calm enough to talk through the problem. Effective listening skills and the acknowledgment that there is a problem are key ingredients to gaining control of a bad situation. Maintaining control then helps to keep your customer calm. Anger, frustration, and high stress levels cloud the clarity of what you say and what you hear.

If customers think you are not listening to the problem, their agitation will increase. Here are some helpful steps to effective listening:

- Eliminate all other distractions and focus your attention on your customer.
- Do not interrupt the customer to answer the phone.
- Do not read paperwork or count money.
- Nod your head periodically.
- Use quiet phrases, such as "yes" or "uh-huh," so that your customer knows you are listening.
- Don't join the customer's tirade.

Agreeing with a customer's *negative emotions* will only heighten those emotions, so avoid joining the complaint session. Remember that in customers' minds, listening equals believing, and your attentiveness validates their emotions.

Often customers simply want someone to know there is a problem. By acknowledging the problem, you are empowering them and diffusing a difficult situation. To acknowledge what customers perceive the problem to be, reflect what you understand they are telling you. Then acknowledge that it is a problem.

Acknowledgment is as simple as saying "Yes, that is a problem." It doesn't require that anyone shoulder the blame; it only recognizes that there is a problem a customer wants or needs to have solved. Project empathy or understanding to customers, and they will find no reason to remain angry.

Until you are in control of the situation, you can do nothing to make customers feel more at ease. Disarm customers, and you can gain control. Customers come to you with expectations about how you will react. All it takes to disarm customers is to respond in a way that they don't expect you to respond. Perhaps you can help them see past the problem, or you can take full blame. Sometimes all it takes is to agree with the customer.

If agreeing that there is a problem doesn't work, there are other options you can use to help you gain control. Using humor is a good one, especially if you can turn a derogatory remark toward you into a joke.

Whatever method you use, give your customer something unexpected and you will have the upper hand.

Once you have gained control of the situation, it is imperative that you maintain that control. Maintaining control happens only when you act in a proactive manner. Ask yourself, "What does this customer need and how can I provide it?" When you focus on customers' needs, then you can focus on the problem, not the emotions. When you know what the problem is, you can provide a solution rather than reacting to customers' anger or frustration.

Customers Want Their Problem Solved

Contrary to popular belief, most of your customers are not looking for something for nothing; they come to you with a sense of fair play. Their sense of fair play includes the expectation that you will also play fair. That means that customers expect you to help without falling back on policy as an excuse not to provide a solution.

Negotiating a winning situation includes:

- Learning what the customer expects as a solution.
- Exploring alternative solutions if necessary.
- Taking control of providing the solution the customer wants.

Don't assume you know what customers want. The best way to provide the solution customers expect is to ask them what they would like you to do. However, this is a technique that should be handled carefully. When asked in the wrong tone of voice, the question "What would you like me to do about this?" can sound crass and sarcastic.

A better way to learn what solution customers expect is to ask:

- "How would you like me to solve this problem?"
- "What would make this situation better for you?"

In the event that you cannot provide the solution that a customer expects, suggest alternatives, and come to a mutual agreement on the solution you will provide.

Sometimes there is no way to give a customer exactly what he expects from you. But you can probably meet the customer halfway. It may take more than one suggestion to find a solution that makes the customer happy. Use this situation as an opportunity to provide service above and beyond what the customer expects.

Sometimes it's necessary to hand a customer off to another person to provide the solution to her problem. Even if that is the case, you can take an active role in solving the customer's problem, and it remains your responsibility to ensure that a solution is reached in a timely and efficient manner.

Once you agree on a solution, you should set in motion the steps necessary to make the customer happy. Remember, it's the small things you do—such as personally explaining the problem to the next person the customer will deal with—that provide the atonement that the customer expects.

Dealing with challenging customers over the phone is even more difficult than dealing with them in person. To make matters worse, the customer has frequently already invested a significant amount of time on the phone by the time the call comes to you. Between holding, going through the voice menu system, and having to recite his account number to you *once again* (even though he just punched in the whole number on the voice mail system minutes ago), he's pretty worked up. When you can't see your customers, you can't judge your progress by their body language, and customers can't judge your intent by your body language. That's reason enough to monitor your tone of voice.

Here are some rules to adhere to when dealing with customers over the telephone:

- Don't place a customer on hold needlessly.

- Don't transfer customers into never-never land.
- Use the same manners that you would in person.

Since customers can't view your reactions over the telephone, they will pay special attention to the tone of your voice.

If there is no way to avoid putting a customer on hold, explain why you are doing so, and ask her permission to activate the hold button. Asking "Can you hold, please?" leaves customers feeling as if they have no choice in the matter. Instead, try "May I put you on hold for just a moment?" Then listen to the answer that customers give rather than cutting them off with the hold button.

Aside from being put on hold, one of the most irritating situations for customers is being transferred from one person to the next, and having to explain their problems repeatedly. Try to solve each customer's problem on your own. If you must transfer a customer, be sure to explain the problem to the next person yourself.

Ideally, you should include the customer in the call as you explain the problem to the person who will work to amend the situation. If that's not possible, explain to the next customer service representative what the problem is in detail. The fewer times customers are forced to repeat their problem, the less likely it is that their anger will grow.

The telephone has become a thorn in the side of customers who have to contact companies. By using impeccable telephone manners, you can disarm challenging customers before they even get started. Manners—such as saying *please* and *thank you*, and not interrupting—are just as important as when you are speaking with customers face to face. Use the same manners on the telephone that you would use if customers could see you.

Customers Are Always Right

Customer service rules that have circulated for years still apply.

Rule #1 The customer is always right.

Rule #2 If the customer is wrong, refer to Rule 1.

That the customer is always right doesn't mean that the customer is never wrong. It simply means that the customer should never be made to *feel* wrong. Among the many things that you should *not* tell customers is that they're wrong. Telling customers that they are wrong, even if it's true, embarrasses them. This embarrassment serves only to increase their agitation. Instead, work to find a suitable solution for the problem without assigning blame to anyone. Also, avoid making customers feel guilty about the problem.

Take their problems as your own, not in terms of blame or responsibility but in terms of solution. In some cases, that means you'll have to avoid the whole issue of who is to blame. In other cases, it means that you need to remove the blame that a customer is feeling. To do that, gloss over the blame and go straight for the solution. Own the problem and you own the solution.

After an outburst or upon realizing that they have made a mistake, customers may begin to feel embarrassed. Help them to feel dignified through the conclusion of the situation by maintaining your professional demeanor. Be empathetic about the situation. Empathy is an essential skill that is required when dealing with anyone, especially a challenging customer. Being empathetic requires that you listen, understand, and attempt to make the customer feel more comfortable with the outcome of the situation.

Remove the issue of blame and get to the heart of solving the problem. No one wins the blame game. The problem is the issue, and the solution to the problem is all that matters.

Follow Up and Follow Through

Many people assume that once a problem has been solved or passed on, it no longer belongs to them. However, this is far from the truth. Once you have finished with a customer, you should take personal responsibility for seeing that your customer is favorably impressed.

Here are a few steps to ensuring good service:

- Check to ensure that your organization has responded properly to the problem.
- Ensure that the customer is pleased with the solution.
- Provide an alternative solution if necessary.
- Take the opportunity to learn from experiences with challenging customers.

Only then can you be assured that your customer has received the best service that your organization can give.

You may not be the person who handles the solution to your customer's problem. However, you should ensure that the solution is implemented. Even if you have to transfer the customer to someone else to solve the problem, you should follow up with the other customer service representative to ensure that a suitable solution was reached. *Internal follow-up is essential to tracking and solving recurring problems.*

You should also contact the customer to ensure that the final solution was reasonable and acceptable to him or her. After the fact, the customer may still be unhappy with the solution. Many customers are afraid to complain a second time if they don't feel satisfied with the solution. The customer may still not be satisfied once a resolution has taken place. Follow up to be sure satisfaction has been provided. Contact your customer again and ask his opinion of the outcome of the situation. Use a phrase such as, "I just wanted to apologize again, and make sure that you received the solution you expected." A comment like this should encourage customers to talk about their opinion of the outcome.

A simple follow-up call takes only a few minutes, and it will determine whether the customer is satisfied with the solution. You may learn that the customer was not satisfied with the solution. It may be that he expected a better or different solution. Or it may be that he is still angry about the mistake. Whatever the case may be, the follow-up call will help to ensure your customer's satisfaction.

Both you and your customer may have agreed on a solution, but the customer may not feel that the problem has been resolved. You should be prepared to offer an alternative solution if necessary.

An alternative solution can be as simple as going one step further, or it may require that you back up and begin the solution process over again. Ask the customer what solution she would have liked to receive or would like to receive now. Then do everything in your power to provide that solution.

Also, work to ensure that the customer feels your company has atoned for its perceived wrongdoings by offering a little "something more." It could be a small gift or discount, as long as it is given in sincerity. The point is to make your customers feel that they are important to your organization.

Challenging customers offer you the opportunity to learn to better serve other customers and to resolve problems within your organization before they become issues. It is your job to ensure that management is aware of those problems.

Once you have provided a satisfactory solution to customers, your job is not over. You need to report the problem to a member of management or a customer service team that is responsible for reporting on customer problems. Doing this prevents the problem from occurring for other customers in the future.

In some companies, teams of customer service representatives are responsible for tracking difficulties with customers from beginning to end. These teams then report to upper management on the problems and how they can be prevented in the future.

If your company doesn't have that kind of a team, take responsibility for reporting the problems to your supervisor. Also, approach the supervisor with a suggestion for preventive action that will keep the problem from occurring again.

Summary

Customer service is the ability of an organization to consistently meet the needs of customers. Good customer service creates goodwill and workforce satisfaction and results in satisfied customers who would return for more services or recommend your financial services company to others.

The first step in effective customer service is to determine exactly what the wants and needs of customers are. To do this, you can focus on the customers who have the highest lifetime value to your company or those who comprise the largest categories among your customer base.

Customer service techniques such as quality circles, workgroups, and service-level standards are some of the ways of executing customer service initiatives. Service-level standards provide ways to quantify whether service is being provided as planned. To determine whether a customer service program is achieving its goals, you must be able to measure and track outcomes.

The best companies place customers at the center of their efforts. They develop a service-focused culture, and they seek and accept feedback from employees. A service-focused culture recognizes that customer satisfaction is the result of good customer service, identifies employees as the crucial element in successful service, and emphasizes that the only goals that can be reached are those that enjoy the investment of the entire workforce.

To ensure continuous improvement, these circular activities should be ongoing: needs assessments, employee training, integration into the performance process, outcomes measurement, and feedback. Continuous improvement refers to the need to follow up on any activities intended to create change and to continue assessing needs and gathering feedback when undertaking customer service initiatives.

Summary

In spite of good customer service, there will be times you are faced with a difficult or challenging customer. It is important to remember that customers who are angry or upset want their problem heard, want an apology, and want to have their problem solved. Listen carefully and remember that it is not personal; the customer is upset at the situation, not at you.

Negotiating a winning solution includes learning what the customer expects, exploring alternative solutions if necessary, and taking control of providing the solution the customer wants.

Dealing with a challenging customer on the telephone is even more difficult. Some rules to help are: Don't place customers on hold needlessly, don't transfer them into "never-never" land, and use the same manners you would in person. Also, watch your tone of voice and keep calm. Finally, report to management anything you learned that would help your organization improve customer service.

CHAPTER 11

Context and Content: Putting It All Together

After reading this chapter, you will be able to:

- Understand the importance of the context and content of information.
- Apply this book's key objectives to your responsibilities.
- Demonstrate a stronger sense of how the key concepts build on one another.
- Make good decisions through context-driven thinking.

Mastering the Business of Banking

Gaining mastery of the business of banking requires that you, the banker, learn a vast amount of information—such as the information you have studied in this book. This chapter will reinforce what you've learned and provide a simple road map for successfully integrating this information into your day-to-day activities.

Context versus Content—What Does This Mean?

For true mastery to take place, you must do more than embrace new concepts. You must also learn how to apply the concepts or information you have learned to your day-to-day responsibilities with confidence for a successful outcome. Learning more about context versus content will help you to do this.

Content represents the *what* of information. It is the factual information. *Context* represents the framework, circumstance, or setting of the information. Put another way, content is the message, context is the medium. Change the context of a message, and you change the meaning of the message.

If you've ever watched late-night TV, you might have noticed that one of the ways talk-show hosts get huge laughs is by using real newspaper or magazine ads or headlines. Usually innocent people placed these ads and headlines, not realizing the "context" of their communication.

Here is an example. Picture yourself suffering from insomnia and paging through your local newspaper. You come across an ad for a sleep aid with the headline. "Never again wake up in the middle of the night!" You read on and make a decision to ask your doctor about prescribing this medication.

Now, picture the same scenario, only this time you are reading the obituaries. You see the same headline. What is the first thing that comes to mind? A sleep aid that you might be interested in? Not likely. Probably your first thought is about someone dying in the middle of the night. The same message, different context, different outcome.

Context and Your Job

Now, how does this concept of context versus content described here apply to you? What have you learned that applies to your job? The concept that new information needs to be processed is easy to understand, but sometimes taking that information and making it relevant in your day-to-day work is more difficult. But it can be done—with practice! Here are some ideas:

As you go about your day-to-day activities, get in the habit of noticing the settings, circumstances, and other contextual information available to you. Then consider the factual information you have recently learned, think about the specific circumstance you are experiencing and how the two might be related, and integrate it in your mind. You are now ready to make a judgment as to the best course of action in each unique situation.

Take time to think about the underlying business issues your bank policies and procedures are attempting to address. Ascertain the meaning of new regulations and the impact of a rapidly changing world in implementing change in your bank.

Get in the habit of seeing the "big picture" while executing tactically. Let decisions be driven by the context of the challenge. Doing this will help you to see the business of banking in a new light and ensure that you make better decisions across the board.

Do not completely ignore the conventional wisdom of focusing on terms, definitions, and textbook-oriented information. Rather, look for balance between the logical content and the contextual application.

Contextual decision making takes practice, but to operate in a highly regulated, profit-centric, and people-driven business, you will need the extra edge it will give you.

You have begun this process in this book. By focusing on factual material while training yourself to think through everyday issues from a practical standpoint, this skill develops naturally.

Summary of Key Concepts

This book has focused on the regulatory environment, discussed the essential components of the business of banking, and incorporated the often-overlooked but critical people aspect of banking. Doing so has included looking at ethical considerations of the banker, as an employee, supervisor, and business developer, and in other customer-facing roles. We learned how to deal with difficult customers, supervise others, and develop new business.

The book introduced you to the business of banking. You have covered all the necessary material to be confident with "what everyone needs to know, do, and understand about banking."

Today more than ever before, financial services professionals need to understand both the highly regulated environment they function in and the highly entrepreneurial environment in which even once-staid banks must operate today. Because it lays the groundwork so effectively, this book helps you to build confidence and gain a firm grasp of essentials and the tools to apply that knowledge. By reading this book, you have gained information that is part of required regulatory training as well as information useful in building a competitive edge.

Online Tools

For more information on these and other topics, please go to www.smartpros.com, where you'll find a library of online courses covering topics in this book as well as many others. Online learning is a great way to build mastery on your own schedule. Each topic covered in this course is available in a companion online course.

Index

C

D

E

F

T

W

1792 95